# An Estate Car Named Desire

# AN ESTATE CAR NAMED DESIRE

## A Life on the Road

MARTIN GURDON

Duckworth Overlook

First published in the UK and the US in 2016 by
Duckworth Overlook

LONDON
30 Calvin Street, London E1 6NW
T: 020 7490 7300
E: info@duckworth-publishers.co.uk
www.ducknet.co.uk
For bulk and special sales please contact
sales@duckworth-publishers.co.uk, or write to us at the above address.

The right of Martin Gurdon to be identified as the Author of the Work has
been asserted by him in accordance with the Copyright, Designs
and Patents Act 1988.
A catalogue record for this book is available from the British Library.

ISBN:
UK: 978–0–7156–5035–6
Typeset by Ian Bahrami

Printed and bound in Denmark by Nørhaven

# Contents

# Acknowledgements

Thanks to Andrew Lockett, Nikki Griffiths, Deborah Blake, Peter Mayer and everyone at Duckworth. Also Phil Willson of the Triumph Sports Six Club and Neil Lyndon. Special thanks to Giles Chapman for sensitive use of the blue pencil. Love to Sheila Ableman and thanks for knocking on the right door. Love also to David, my dad, who's lived with most of this stuff and still speaks to me, and finally to Jenny, his wife, and Jane, my wife, who've lived with some of it and have now put up with my writing about it.

# Hard Shoulder to Cry On

'Have they broken down yet?'

This was usually the first thing Aunt Sheila said to Aunt Pat when she phoned to see where we'd got to on the journey between London and Lancashire. In the late 1960s our annual family holidays were a nostalgia trip and an escape from London for my mother, who'd grown up in the now extinct county of Westmorland, which has long since been eaten by Cumbria. Every year we'd make a pilgrimage to the pretty market town of Kirkby Stephen, where my mum had spent part of her childhood before and during the last war. We'd stay about sixty miles away with Aunt Pat, one of her sisters, whose family lived in a 1930s semi in Goosnargh, a large village not far from Preston.

This pleasantly bourgeois house, with a garage whose wooden doors were decorated with a sunburst pattern, and contained an Austin Cambridge, seemed a very long way from where we lived in London; especially as my dad's cars tended to prolong the journey by expiring. This used to irritate the hell out of my mother, but to me was part of the adventure. I did not pick up on the parental vibes, liked being in the back of one of dad's aged Jowett Javelins, watching the scenery, the other cars, trucks and coaches, and was as happy to do this when we were stuck by the roadside with the bonnet up as when we were moving.

When I was a baby, my dad had owned a rackety Ford 10, whose gearbox began to make a 'tap-tap-tap' noise en route to

3

Lancashire. This developed into 'knock-knock-knock,' and by the time we got there it was going 'bang!-bang!-bang!' The box had also given up engaging top gear. Up on a ramp at a local garage my dad and a taciturn mechanic looked ruefully at the grey fluid dribbling from its gearbox oil filler plughole. Mixed with metal filings from some internal part that was being ground to death, were bits of gearwheel teeth.

'Can't fix that until next week,' said the mechanic.

My dad said he had to go back to work, couldn't wait, so if the gearbox could be filled with fresh oil then he'd grind his way south without the benefit of top gear.

'If that gets you home,' said the mechanic, 'I'll show you my bollocks.'

Forty-eight hours later he received a phone call. It was my dad, exhausted, but back in our house.

'Get polishing,' he said.

My mother and I did not travel with him, instead heading south a few days later on the amusingly named 'Gay Hostess' double-decker coaches that used to travel the M1 between Preston's new brutalist bus terminus and London's art deco coach station in Victoria.

Launched in 1959, these cream and red Leyland Atlanteans had thundering rear engines, toilets that made comedy sucking noises, and a serving hatch where tea, food, and fags were sold by hosts and hostesses. The idea was that coach passengers could have an airline-like experience between Preston and London, as they wafted along at 64mph. With their soft high-backed seats and shiny interiors the Atlanteans were the acme of excitement for a vehicle-obsessed four-year-old. We would sit upstairs and watch changing rural and urban landscapes slip by.

I don't remember my dad's Ford, but his first Jowett Javelin was very much part of our lives. In the 1930s, Jowett had been a slightly stodgy little car maker, operating from the Yorkshire town of Idle, near Bradford, which is quite an entertaining place name for somewhere that made cars. Its most famous offering was probably a van called the Bradford, which had a tough 'flat twin' engine that gave it the tenacity of a mountain goat, hauling this little tin box up and down the steep roads of its native Yorkshire Dales. The puttering, parochial Bradford was very much for local consumption, and in the mid 1940s Jowett's bosses realised that if it was to survive the company needed a modern and export-friendly car, so it hired an ingenious engineer called Gerald Palmer, and told him to get on with designing it. Palmer was inspired by the 1937 Lancia Aprilia saloon, which like today's cars had a 'unitary construction' body that did away with a chassis frame, so was all one piece. The Lancia featured independent suspension and a host of other technically clever ideas that many cars lacked thirty years later.

Palmer came up with a wind-cheating, quite rakish four-door saloon that vaguely resembled a scaled-down 1930s American gangster's car, but like the Lancia had a strong, light, chassisless body that seated six. It also had rack-and-pinion steering that was very accurate, ingenious 'torsion bar' suspension to help it go round corners and a 1,500cc 'flat four' engine, whose components moved from side to side rather than up and down. This meant the engine sat lower in the car, helping the Javelin's weight distribution, and again, the handling. In a world where many bigger cars struggled to hit 70mph, this technical tour de force could cruise for hours at nearly 10mph faster, and had the dynamic poise to win its class on the Monte Carlo Rally.

The Javelin should have been a world-beater, but as with so many clever British cars the quality of its conception was not matched by the quality of its construction, and Javelins went wrong, with their gearboxes being a particular weakness. After a while, Jowett decided to build them itself rather than buy them from an outside supplier, but didn't do this properly, so its factory became clogged with broken transmissions, and in 1954 Jowett went bust, buried under an avalanche of warranty claims.

This didn't stop my dad appreciating the Javelin's design, so in 1968 he bought one, loved it when it went, and put up with it when it went wrong, which was often. I was probably about four when this car made the annual journey north for the first time. We set off very early in the morning. Wrapped in blankets, I was laid across the leather back seat and told to lie down and sleep. My recollections of the journey have the quality of an old colour ciné film, and mostly involve looking up at the sky. It was pitch black and I watched the big street lamps on Kew Bridge slide by over my head, their yellow cube shapes standing out against the darkness. At the bottom of the bridge we'd turn right, and the lamps swung on an invisible axis as the car shouldered the bend and made for the Chiswick roundabout. Soon afterwards I drifted into sleep.

When I woke the sky had a weak, early dawn light. We'd stopped at a service station, and my parents were talking quietly. Listening to their voices rising and falling I looked at the station's illuminated totem, which had a stylised motif of a head in profile with a winged helmet. What did it mean?

Naturally we broke down later during the journey. We'd left the motorway and had been barrelling along a busy A road, in the company of Morris Minors and flashier Ford Cortinas and Vauxhall Victors. Exiting a roundabout the Jowett made a strange noise, a kind of metallic scything sound. My father uttered a strange word that I didn't understand, but my mother did, which caused her to say something to him that seemed to add to an already tense atmosphere as the Jowett coasted into a lay-by. Dad clambered wearily out of the car and hauled up the bonnet. The Javelin rocked a bit as he did something mysterious, which involved muffled muttering and cursing.

Back in the car he announced that a cooling fan blade had sheered off and embedded itself in the radiator. He'd left it there to stop all the coolant leaking out, but with three blades left the fan was out of balance and we would have to progress very slowly to the nearest garage for repairs, and hope that the inevitable coolant leak would be slow enough for us to make it before the car boiled dry.

My mother offered him a cigarette. 'Guards' was my parents' preferred brand, and soon the Jowett's cabin was hazy with fag smoke as the car tottered back on to the road and trundled slowly along it, with a queue of traffic forming behind. Luckily we found a garage, where my mother headed for a nearby callbox to tell her sister that we would be late, and my dad discussed tactics with a man in oil-stained blue overalls.

In the hours that followed, my mother went to sleep in the front of the car. I sat in the back and stared at the inside of the workshop, its walls lined with tools that did God knows what, as the gashed radiator was removed and soldered up, and another fan was sourced from a pile of wrecked cars at the back of the garage, then modified to fit ours.

This sort of thing seemed perfectly normal. Cars broke, especially on long journeys, and a childhood game employed by many parents to keep their offspring quiet was to count the number of dead ones stuck by the roadside.

It was getting dark when we finally got going again, and I nodded off to sleep. The next time I woke the car was parked in the drive of a strange house, and a middle-aged woman whom I didn't recognise, but looked a little like my mother, was scooping me out of the car and carrying me into the house. This was my Aunt Pat. I generally found being 'handled' by adults who weren't my parents alarming, but something about this maternal person made the encounter perfectly natural, so I didn't scream into her face.

I met a short, ruddy-faced man with a bulbous nose and lined features that were slightly forbidding, but who spoke with a warm, Northern voice that wasn't. This was Uncle Mick. Their children, a gangling boy of fourteen called Stephen, and his sister Judith, who had a frizz of hair, and was around four years younger, viewed us with mild interest but then went back to whatever they'd been doing before.

'What was the trouble this time?' asked Aunt Pat, during a post-mortem of our journey down from London.

Later the conversation was repeated with a second woman whom we'd gone to visit. She looked very much like Aunt Pat and my mum. This was their sister Aunt Sheila (why were they both called 'Aunt'?), who ran a Post Office with Uncle Bob, a grey-haired jovial man who drove a low-slung stylish Wolseley 4/44, which sounded rather sporting and had a wood and leather interior. Years later I discovered that Gerald Palmer had designed this car too, and that when the apparently genial Bob had first clapped eyes on my dad, the dark red smoking jacket he'd been wearing made him question his future brother-in-law's sexuality.

The 'break down' conversation became a feature of successive visits to both households. Every summer we'd set off full of hope, the Jowett would die and we'd arrive late. Once Aunt Pat and Uncle Mick came to London in their Austin Cambridge, a stolid, square-rigged thing painted black, with soft, comfortable red leather seats. We drove in it to Crystal Palace, walked amongst the giant models of dinosaurs that were relics of the Great Exhibition, and whose plodding solidity reminded me of the car, then drove home along streets made up of strange cube-shaped single-storey houses that my mother said were 'Prefabs.'

My father was missing from this party and mostly absent the rest of the time, being engaged in a mysterious adult activity called 'work'. So when Aunt Pat and Uncle Mick journeyed north he stayed in London, but my mother and I went with them, sitting in the back of the Austin in tight formation with my cousins, as we trundled up the M1 at a steady 65mph. The Austin covered the 230-odd miles without breaking down, which was a revelation.

I liked the Cambridge, from its friendly engine note to the little green light that flashed at the end of its single indicator stalk. My mother liked the fact that it didn't go wrong, and unflattering comparisons were drawn.

Perhaps my dad remembered those words on our next trip north when, some way up the M1, the Jowett's exhaust tried parting company from the rest of the car. The Javelin had good ground clearance, which, once we'd rolled to a farting halt in the corner of a vast concrete motorway services car park, allowed him to crawl underneath and effect repairs with an old wire coat hanger. As the sickly car again rocked on its springs and the sound of cursing wafted up through the floorboards, the sky grew dark and it began raining. The gloom made it very difficult for Dad to see. Fortunately he had a torch. This was an expensive, pressed tin, Dalek-shaped 'Pifco' with an adjustable lamp at the front and a red plastic dome at the top, in which was a light that flashed. It should have been ideal, but the main torch bulb had gone, and he had to try and re-attach the exhaust to the car's filthy underside using the flashing red light. What had started as a shower quickly turned into a thunderstorm. Icy rainwater gushed over the car park, under the car and soaked my father, who was serenaded by deafening thunderclaps, but at least the lightning helped him see what he was doing. Perhaps it was this experience that finally persuaded him to buy a different car.

'What is it?' asked Mum.

'Another Jowett Javelin.'

'Oh God.'

This was a younger Javelin, a stripling of just fifteen summers, which meant it was less worn out than its late 1940s predecessor, but had the disadvantage of being fitted with a gearbox that Jowett had made itself, rather than the stronger, 'bought in' box of the older car. The new Javelin's 'homemade' gearbox was a mechanical time bomb waiting to explode, but my dad knew this, and when we next headed north, he packed a spare good box and his tools, and a special engine-removing trolley, along with our holiday luggage.

I can still recall the sound made by the stripping gear teeth and mechanical shrapnel of a Jowett gearbox trying to select two gears at once. This happened about fifty miles from Preston after my dad foolishly decided to engage third gear. The metallic shattering went on for a very long time. Once again we arrived at Aunt Pat and Uncle Mick's after dark, on the end of a towrope. My dad spent the first two days of his holiday fitting the new gearbox.

I think my mother grew to actively hate Jowett Javelins, and perhaps this piece of mechanical betrayal finally persuaded her husband that she had a point, so in about 1970 he spent £150 on a sixteen-foot-long Bristol 401. This was a slippery bodied, hump-backed two-door saloon with push buttons instead of door handles and a six-cylinder, two-litre engine that was 'a little tired.' My dad said this car resembled 'the arse end of a well sucked boiled sweet.' I thought it looked sinister and that I wouldn't like it, before discovering that it had huge personality and charm.

The Bristol became 'the car I wanted when I grow up,' but was not without its quirks. This one had been given a cheap respray, and the paint had taken against its aluminium hand-beaten bodywork, forming scabs and dropping off it. Instead of flashing indicators the Bristol had 'trafficators.' These were plastic semaphore arms with little lights in them. Located in recesses inside the driver and passenger door pillars, these jerked to attention to let the rest of the world know your direction of travel, and had a habit of sticking. When sitting in the back I was often instructed to thump the inside of the pillars to make them flop home again.

The car's interior had a fuselage-like quality and the mechanically cultured series of noises it made were utterly distinctive. In a world of Hillmans, Vauxhalls and Austins it was special, and I knew it.

As for the Jowett, it went out in a blaze of glory. My dad's mysterious work was as a television props and special effects man, working for an ITV company called London Weekend on programmes like *On the Buses* and *Upstairs Downstairs*. He'd been asked to find an old car for a sketch about dodgy vehicle dealers, featuring Michael Palin as a motor trade spiv and Graham Chapman as his victim.

Sprayed a lurid pea green, the family Javelin was donated as the sacrificial car, and rigged up so that on cue, my dad, who was hiding in the back, out of shot, pulled on lengths of fishing line so that doors, bumpers, grille and other bits fell off at strategic moments as Palin's pencil moustached chancer insisted the car was perfect. The Javelin achieved this self-destruction with complete reliability.

The programme featured most of the Monty Python team, and the car item was, allegedly, the inspiration for Python's Dead Parrot sketch. Today you can find our Jowett's very public demise on YouTube, where it's been watched nearly 800,000 times.

When she was watching the car dropping to bits on national television, I wonder if my mum thought the name of the programme appropriate.

It was 'How to Irritate People.'

# Wheel Nut

Did I leave sticky finger marks? If so, the owner of the MGB sportscar never complained.

The car was a Roadster, which meant it had an open roof, which was often folded away during the summer. It was painted a sober mid blue, which rather suited it, and after the parade of family saloons and estates that preceded it on the journey my mother and I made to the shops, its neatly low, wide, curving shape stood out. The man who owned the MG lived on the same late Victorian street in the South West London suburb as we did, so it was a fixture of my early life, and by default, my mother's too.

In 1967, when I was almost four years old, that journey could be protracted, because I loved cars and was keen to stop and take in everything about them: Ford Anglias had metallic eyebrows and chrome-grilled grimaces. The back window of an Austin Cambridge, painted the colour of red wine gums, was deeply curved and I would always peer through it at the slightly distorted houses on the other side of the road. There were a lot of Minis, painted primary colours that reminded me of the balloons my parents had bought at Christmas. Although still taller than me, Minis were low enough to the ground to see inside, look at the levers, switches and instruments, and wonder at the alchemy that made them work.

Although still almost illiterate and innumerate, I'd begun to recognise the outlines and script of the badges, sometimes running stubby fingers along chrome hieroglyphs that spelt out

'Triumph,' 'Fiat,' 'Austin,' 'Morris.' I knew all the names even if I had yet to connect them to their letter shapes.

The differences between these often almost identical cars intrigued me too. Why did some have more dials or gearlevers in different places? Why the variety of chrome side-flashes and other decorations? Inured to the hierarchies and status these implied to a lot of adults, even in the late 1960s, I found them a source of interest rather than aspiration or envy. I wanted to know more, but was quite happy to wait before I found out.

Half way down the street was a curious little car. My dad had said approvingly that it was a Riley Elf, which I had worked out was a slightly mutant Mini. What I didn't understand was that a lot of cars with different names were made by the same nebulous conglomerates, as a result of mergers that had seen once independent firms climb into bed with each other. Their products were often becoming interchangeable bar their names and arcane detailing.

This process of dilution was known as 'badge engineering,' and it meant that many Austins, Morrises, Rileys and Wolseleys were related to an incestuous degree, and explained why the little Riley Elf was really just a Mini hiding behind some Pooterish, bourgeois upgrades. Outside it had grown a stumpy boot that stuck out like a bustle. Inside it smelt different from other Minis, which had strong, not unpleasant odours of mass-produced plastics and vinyls particular to cars of this period. The Elf had a tang of libraries and the jackets my dad often wore, because its seats were trimmed in leather, with bright red borders and square cream inserts.

Standard Minis had stark dashboards with big round speed-ometers stuck in the middle like mantelpiece clocks. Some were encased in eye-shaped oval binnacles with a couple of extra gauges on either side to tell you how much petrol was left and how hot the engine was getting. The Riley Elf had the three instruments, but the whole dash was encased in veneered wood panelling of the sort used on the valve radios many families, including ours, still owned.

The car's nose also set it apart. Other Minis had rounded, snub fronts with bug-eyed headlamps and half elliptical grilles that looked like downturned mouths. The Elf appeared fussier but less startled, with a snout whose centre contained a rectangular chrome grille, dipping at the top to accommodate an enamelled diamond-shaped blue maker's badge, rounded at the corners and tapering towards its lower edges. This was a cut price homage to the sort of decorative front ends most cars had worn thirty years before, and was flanked on either side by chrome strips that ran horizontally towards the indicators, like bristling, shining moustaches.

The Elf was painted red, except for its roof, which was white, like icing on a cake, and lacked the cheerfully tasteless pizzazz of the two-tone Fords and Vauxhalls which shared the street with it. The way their paint schemes changed half way up their bodies reminded me of the pink and yellow wafer biscuits my mother bought, or the confectionery that was my heart's desire.

For a child who still interpreted the world in a sensory as well as linguistic way, these were positive associations. They represented things I liked, and if seeing the ordinary cars on our street was as pleasurable as dipping into a bag of sweets and savouring the differences between them, then the MGB Roadster was the equivalent of eating a rocket-shaped Zoom ice lolly. The Zoom came in three sugary flavours and colours and was a special treat. Consuming it had a slightly ritualistic feel. So did giving the MG a childish once over.

To see inside it I had to stand on my toes and peer over the door into the cabin and inhale the scents of the sun-baked black leather seats and black leatherette soft top that was hot when you touched it. I'd peer into the crackle-finished black metal dashboard with its jumbled array of round dials and glinting, chromed outer edges, and the rotary dials in the middle that could have come from a domestic gas cooker.

Did I lean over and clasp the black rim of the steering wheel with pudgy fingers? Perhaps. I had no sense of personal space or ownership, but I do remember that the steering wheel had slim bicycle-wheel spokes in three rows that formed a kind of 'ban the bomb' shape.

That MG seemed huge, as all cars did, but as with them I saw something benign in its shape, although being a sportscar it would, I knew, be frighteningly, but irresistibly fast.

This was a car with a voice: its engine note, a deep powerful burble, was as distinct to me as the voices of my parents and friends, but then a lot of other cars had voices too. Triumph Heralds purred, Rover 100s, the ones with St Bernard dog profiles, made a soft, almost musical whining sound when setting off sedately from traffic lights, Morris Minors blew flatulent raspberries when they slowed down. I'd hear these things and assumed other people did too. I read facial features and characteristics into the mass-produced vehicles that cluttered the road on that regular shopping journey. Often I didn't need to see cars to know what they were. The sound they made was enough to identify them, and I felt entirely at home in their company and believed that they possessed distinctive personalities. So perhaps it's not surprising that I thought that they must be alive.

My mother, chain-smoking, neatly diminutive, keen on ballet, music, reading, would eventually take my hand firmly, and walk briskly towards the pond, the green, the shops and the repetition of visiting the butcher, the greengrocer, the cavernous hardware store, the VG Stores supermarket with the chattering cash registers, packets of fish fingers and frozen peas. Each of her adult steps required two of my childish ones to keep up, and I would eventually tire as I was towed along, and grumble because I wanted a rest and because I wanted to see the brown Ford Thames van owned by the builder at the top of the road, the stately Bentley with a grille that resembled a chrome-plated fireplace, or the Heinkel bubble car, with its single door at the front, which just looked funny.

My mother had spent the morning ironing, wanting to get this particular drudge out of the way so that she could paint in the afternoon. Preoccupied and bored, she'd burned herself and cursed. Now the triangular red welt on her wrist throbbed. She was, putting it mildly, less engaged with the prospect of trudging round the shops than I was. There were really big supermarkets, with wide, strip-lit aisles, but these were a bus ride away, so we were enmeshed in the ritual of the 'little and often' local shop. Those shops were in a continuous arc of dark brick Victorian terraces, and vibrated to the traffic that moved sludgily past them on the South Circular road, and was the cause of more delay as I gawped at huge juddering trucks and friendly-looking, red and rounded double-decker buses. There were plans to knock the shops down and widen the road, something neither of my parents approved of, but this was an era when demolition equalled progress.

About ten minutes after I'd peered at the MG, my mother pulled me into the VG Stores, let go of my hand and went in search of the fish fingers and frozen peas. This was modern, regular-shaped food that came out of packets. Dinner forged from the white fish of technology, or something like that.

As my mother dropped things into a wire basket I wandered off and found a huge display of soup tins, which started at floor level and triangulated to a point some way above my head. I sat down, thud, and contemplated this edifice. By then my mother had moved to the other end of the shop and was hunting for Oxo Cubes when she heard the crash caused by my pulling a tin from the bottom of the display.

The noise was loud and prolonged. Fearing the worst she ran back down the aisle to find two old ladies in woolly greatcoats. They had cartoon horror faces and were staring at her son, who was sitting cross-legged on the floor, surrounded by soup tins. At intervals I would select one and hurl it up the aisle. The distances weren't great, but long enough for me to intone 'F**k!' and 'B*****y!' with each throw.

Clearly my receptive language was improving, and I must have heard when she'd been burned by the iron and sworn.

Years later she'd remind me of her excruciating embarrassment, how she hadn't smacked me, although the idea was immensely appealing, and how she thought my pensionable audience had thoroughly enjoyed their censorious disapproval.

'I'm tired!' I moaned as we marched home, my mother holding my wrist in a firm grip with one hand, and taking a longed-for drag from a cigarette with the other. We didn't stop to look at the cars we'd seen on the way to the shops, which seemed odd to me.

'Not now,' said my mother as she tugged me past the blue MG.

When the dull throb of her ironing burn had receded, along with the sense of parental humiliation, she'd thought:

'At least he was thinking about something other than bloody cars.'

# Evil on Wheels

When I was six I knew evil when I saw it, and generally evil wore a beard.

This was largely thanks to Lew Grade, whose Associated Television company spent much of the 1960s and '70s churning out gaudy adventure and detective series like *The Saint* and *The Persuaders*, which starred Roger Moore. Grade also bankrolled Gerry Anderson's *Supercar, Captain Scarlett and the Mysterons* and *Thunderbirds*, which we rarely seemed to watch at home, and I usually only saw with my friend Jamie, who lived over the road. All these shows appeared on ITV, or 'commercial television,' which even as a small boy I sensed was a bit racier than the BBC. ITV's entertainingly vulgar sagas were sandwiched between flickering advertisements involving the Milk Tray man and his careful hair leaping out of helicopters, or people singing about washing powder. There was also the housewife reversing her aged Austin A30 into a frothing, moustached colonel-type's Bentley. The pair then burst into song with the words, 'Nuts! Whole hazelnuts. Oooo! Cadbury's take them and they cover them in chocolate!' (something which became a primary school playground refrain, to be deliciously soiled with rude words).

At the time my experience of primary school was mostly one of bafflement. I knew more about cars than most of my peers, and was able to tell the difference between the then excitingly new Mini Clubman and older snub-nosed Minis, but things like reading, writing, and the boring rituals of something called 'sums' did not penetrate my mind, or if they did would leave it again soon afterward.

Mine was a modern school with modern teaching methods, which included quiet 'reading times.' Once I went to a teacher for some help and made the guileless observation that I'd 'forgotten how to read.'

'Well, you can sit there until you remember,' she said. I'd made her angry and had no idea why. I had genuinely forgotten, but she thought I was being a cheeky, lazy little boy. After that I usually spent the reading periods in a pleasantly fuzzy daze, looking at the pictures in the 'Ant and Bee' books or trying to identify the sounds of passing cars. Was I hearing a Ford Mk1 Cortina or an Anglia?

On paper I could create wonky pencil letter shapes, although often these were hieroglyphs or reversals. I was a copyist with little understanding of what I was copying, and apparently being left-handed somehow related to my difficulties.

'He'll learn when he's ready,' the teachers told my anxious parents. We all waited for this process to start, but as time passed I fell ever further behind. Sometimes this made me feel mildly frustrated, but mostly I just kept quiet to avoid exposure to things I couldn't do, and waited for the eureka moment when, suddenly, I would be able to do them. I was learning more and more about cars, so why not this stuff?

The noise and bustle of school were slightly overwhelming, and as my classmates began to read and write, and I drifted along behind them, I continued to deal with it on a sensory level. The school was a place filled with the noise of scraping chairs, the smell of fresh paint, and the squishy touch of the window putty that never dried, which we were told would be poisonous if we ate it.

School dinners in the clattering canteen were a mixed blessing. Here we ate thin slices of indeterminate meat drowning in lukewarm gravy, or liver, mashed potato igloos with the flavour of fluffed up cardboard, and wet cabbage. Steamed chocolate puddings were popular; slithery, cold tapioca that resembled congealed frogspawn and dairy extract, in the middle of which was a bloodstain red dollop of alleged jam, was not.

I liked playtimes, which were often solitary affairs spent avoiding the bigger children and watching others skipping, playing tag or swapping marbles. I would join in some-times, and enjoyed it when I did, but was quite happy to be an observer. Inevitably, I'd sometimes pretend I was a car. On occasions I was a Wolseley 6/80, which looked a bit like a giant Morris Minor with a big chrome grille, and I'd seen being used as police cars with noisy bells on their front bumpers in the sort of 1950s black and white British crime flicks that starred people like Kenneth More, and were then staples of afternoon TV.

Sometimes I was a veteran car a bit like a Curved Dash Olds-mobile, circa 1900, with giant artillery wheels and tiller steer-ing, that was always difficult to start. In these guises I would happily chug about the playground.

As my fine motor skills, handwriting and reading abili-ties failed to develop I would think of these and other cars as I floated through lessons, or sang extracts of *Jesus Christ Superstar* ('he wears frilly knickers and a see through bra'), or ground through endless explanations about something called 'Decimalization.'

I understood that this meant the appearance of new money and that the big penny and 'thruppeny bit' and 'shilling' coins that jingled in my mother's purse would be replaced by smaller, shinier coinage which would have different values.

'One pound is a hundred new pennies. A hundred new pence to the pound,' we'd chant.

Eventually I was put into Miss Winter's class. She was an unsmiling young woman with a huge fuzzy perm and a taste for violent green dresses to go with her equally virulent green eyeliner. Her pencil eyebrows were the cause of much playground comment. We thought they looked like a pair of brown worms stuck to her face.

She seemed to view us with distaste, a largely mutual feeling not helped by the fact that she talked quickly and became irritated if you didn't keep up. I soon learned to keep my incomprehension to myself, particularly when we began French lessons. I still couldn't spell my name, but learned to parrot approximate noises for the French words Miss Winter wrote on the blackboard, which, of course, I could not read. I knew it didn't matter, as I would learn this stuff when I was ready, and anyway, I knew Renaults and Citroëns came from France.

The things I was learning about cars were irrelevant and distracting, and both these and the little boy 'Nuts! Whole hazelnuts' playground mnemonics that bounced around inside my head were contemptible in the eyes of many grown-ups. Miss Winter was good at contempt, and since we didn't like her, annoying the woman by muttering such things under your breath was irresistible to some of her braver pupils.

The adults we liked sometimes curled their lips at this stuff too, which simply increased its appeal, and when Jamie and I escaped from Miss Winter's strictures and lolled in front of his parent's TV, our antennae for new corruptible advertising jingles were finely honed, as was our appetite for Lew Grade's stylishly schlocky adventure shows. These mostly had villains who shared two characteristics: they were keen on world domination and wore beards. They also did a lot of shouting, usually in heavy German or middle European accents, and although they always lost to the clean-shaven, wisecracking good guys, in ways that I now see indicated extreme ineptitude, as a small child I was entirely in their thrall, often watching them liquidate their victims with pleasurable terror.

However, there was a problem with seeing them do this on Jamie's parents' 'modern' television (modern because although still black and white, it could be tuned to BBC2, something our tiny old Fergusson box was incapable of doing). His dad, George, looked exactly like the mad potentates/industrialists/scientists/criminal masterminds who cackled, threatened and leered out of the screen.

George was huge, barrel-chested and very bearded. Nothing was small about him, from his meaty hands to his booming voice, which could go from a rumble to a roar, and often did. He was also quite shouty, and had a habit of declaiming loudly about life's iniquities. He was often very funny about these things too, spouting stream of consciousness rants, peppered with words I didn't understand, but knew well enough that I'd get into trouble if I used them.

'Sam Goldwyn said there are two types of people in the world: Fuckers or fuckees, and you have to decide which you are. Are you a fuckee or a fucker? Personally I think the world is full of fuckers.'

What, we wondered, would Miss Winter make of the word 'fuckers'?

When George got going, idiocy and stupidity were given wheedling voices and gurning faces. Often I'd have no idea what he was talking about, but found myself laughing at the way it looked and sounded. Oddly, this made him even more alarming. George scared me witless.

Jamie's mother, Elvi, was tiny, but the size difference didn't seem to be a problem to this almost elfin woman with a shock of bright red hair; she smiled a great deal, and was just as noisy as George.

George and Elvi spent a lot of time in their kitchen, often with friends or other people's children, laughing, sparring or rowing pleasurably. My home was quieter and more self-contained, and I liked retreating into it and the company of my parents. My tall, rangy and I now realise rather good-looking dad, David, and Jill, my mother, who was small, short-sighted and vigorous, both loved classical music, and our large-ish home, with its big wooden sash windows, high ceilings and comfortable, elderly furniture and fittings, was often filled with Mozart and Beethoven. We shared the house with a pathologically grumpy tortoiseshell cat, who might have been grumpy because she'd been given the less than original name of 'Puss,' and Sarah, a gentle, deeply stupid Lakeland terrier, who'd been bred as a gun dog but was terrified of explosions. If Jamie and I let off a cap gun Sarah would fling herself into the cupboard under the kitchen sink and quiver, covered in Ajax floor cleaning powder. On one occasion some Dutch friends came to stay, and we all went for a ride in their left-hand drive Volkswagen Variant estate. Nobody was strapped in. We approached some traffic lights that went red, a car backfired and Sarah flung herself into the front footwell between the Volkswagen's terrified driver's foot and the brake pedal. Only by hauling the dog out of the way and skidding to a halt did he prevent us sailing into the middle of a busy road junction.

My parents occasionally made themselves hostages to fortune, and did so this time by saying I could choose Sarah's name.

'Dalek!' I said.

'Think of another one,' they said.

'No. I like Dalek. You said I could choose.'

'You can choose another name.'

'I want to call her Dalek.'

And so on, and so on.

I adored our house, but also enjoyed the contrast with Jamie's nosier home, and as with most of his friends, took George and Elvi's hospitality entirely for granted.

So as Jamie and I watched Roger Moore in Simon Templar guise 'steer' his white Volvo P1800 sports car in front of a suspiciously fake moving background, before decking this week's bearded bad guy with a single punch, the house echoed to George's real life super villain rasp and Elvi's cut-glass ripostes.

Once I asked Jamie what his dad did for a living.

'He works on the telly,' came the reply.

Then I had no idea what my dad did, but not wishing to be outdone, I said that he too worked 'on the telly.' It turned out that we were both telling the truth. George Murcell was an actor. So was his wife. The pair had met when she already had a boyfriend, something to which George strongly objected.

As Elvi cheerfully recalled, the boyfriend was trying to reverse his car out of a car park when George stomped towards them, banged on the bonnet with his fist and shouted:

'You're with the wrong man! It's not him you should be going out with! It's me! Me!'

'I was shouting "Go away!" "Go away!"' said Elvi.

George did not go away, instead appearing at her bedroom window soon afterwards, which was a bit of a surprise, because it was on the second floor. Not long afterwards she gave in and the pair were married noisily and happily for almost forty years.

Like most small boys I was blissfully ignorant, and had no idea that my friend's rumbustious, naughty parents were also socially and culturally sophisticated. In fact, they were artists. George had begun his career with Tyrone Guthrie's touring theatre company, and part of his facility for invective and innuendo-laden verbal flights of fancy came from a love of language and good writing in general and Shakespeare in particular.

The Bard meant nothing to me. My idea of quality drama was Patrick Troughton's Beatles' wig-wearing Doctor Who being chased by a bloke wearing a furry Yeti suit. George had plans to create the first all-Shakespearean theatre in London since the original Globe, but he was also a jobbing actor and bills needed to be paid, so he'd lend his bearded scowl to a series of evil nemesis roles in the sort of TV programmes Jamie and I lapped up with uncritical pleasure.

He was even the voice of 'Master Spy', the bald, jowly middle European puppet bad guy from Gerry Anderson's creaky 'supermarionation' series *Supercar* (the car in question could fly and dive under water, and looked rather like 1950s American dream cars), who often finished sentences with the words 'heh, heh, heh!'

No wonder I found him so alarming.

George drove a huge dark blue and increasingly tatty Humber Hawk saloon, which suited him well. With its expanse of wooden dashboard, wood door cappings and hefty leather seats that were getting worn and tired, the car's interior had a sort of British reserve about it. The outside had a kind of aesthetic schizophrenia, in that it was broad, with bulging extremities, a fair amount of chrome, and 'wrap around' front and rear screens, like many of the late 1950s Chryslers and Chevrolets its stylists were aping. In fact, when it appeared, this was the biggest family saloon car made in Britain, but it was also a car from Coventry rather than Detroit, one that somehow couldn't quite bring itself to embrace the unashamed flashiness of the American vehicles that inspired it.

To me, as a small child, its interior seemed vast. Jamie and I ranged and bounced about on the sagging springs of its enormous rear seat, or sometimes shared the equally voluminous front bench. We never wore seatbelts, which, if they were fitted at all to cars, were fiddly bits of webbing that twisted, tangled and went out of adjustment.

Being in the front of the Humber, nose level with the passenger windows, or peering over the endless curve of its faded blue bonnet, meant sharing space with George, who would hunch bear-like over the Hawk's vast steering wheel, hauling at it to persuade the car's vague steering to point the wheels more or less where he wanted to go, a process that required effort and concentration. Years later I remember talking to someone else who'd owned one of these cars who said that she was never quite sure whether she was in charge of it, or it was in charge of her.

In George's Hawk, the gears were selected by a large metal wand that jutted from the left of the steering column, working the gearbox through a meandering selection of rods and linkages. It was not the acme of precision, and George, who was not tactile when it came to cars, would grab this lever with his fist, like a farmer throttling a chicken, and ram it from ratio to ratio. Although progress never seemed very fast, it wasn't gentle either. Large feet would thump down on clutch, brake and accelerator pedals in such a way that the car's progress tended to involve a series of jerking starts, sudden increases in speed followed by determined stops.

The other distinguishing feature of being driven by George, other than the usually loud invective-filled conversation, was his spatial awareness, which was generally very good, and meant that this giant car would often be threaded through tight traffic gaps without slowing down, or brought to a stop inches from the tailboard of a looming truck.

I came to know some of the owners of the other cars in our street, which tended to be newer and tidier than George's Humber, or indeed my dad's Jowett and the faded blue Bristol that succeeded it. Our next-door neighbour was a nice bloke with tidy hair and a white Peugeot 404 estate. The Peugeot shared a visual neatness with its owner's barnet. He was on an upward career trajectory and in due course the Peugeot was succeeded by a dark green

P6 Rover 3500 saloon. This was a compact, sober-looking thing, which caused my dad some excitement.

'It's got an American V8 engine,' he told me. I was impressed, even though I had no idea what a V8 engine was, although I was quickly aware that the Rover was very powerful and very fast. It certainly sounded expensive.

My dad and the Rover's owner would talk about the car almost every time they met, using mysterious words like 'torque,' which to me sounded like 'talk,' and made me wonder if it might be possible to hold a conversation with the Rover.

An equally neat-looking family who lived across the street drove a smaller, squarer Triumph Herald estate. This dark green car had a grille that grinned, headlamps recessed into deep, chromed bezels that gave it a look of mild surprise, and white rubber edges to its bumpers, which left chalky imprints on your trousers if you rubbed against them, something I did frequently once I'd discovered this.

The Herald people were unusual in that both parents drove. Most of the families I knew consisted of a father who went out to work, often driving there, and a mother who stayed at home and mostly didn't drive. Instinct told me that not everybody lived in this way, but I had yet to meet many people who didn't.

There seemed to be unspoken rules about women not doing stuff. I'd only seen blokes drive taxis and buses and a female newsreader had yet to cross my radar. I knew women could do these things, and vaguely wondered why they didn't, deciding that they would probably get round to it in the bright, shiny future, when life would get even better.

One piece of equality that had arrived involved smoking cigarettes. The sizzle of striking matches, clenched lipped fags-between-the-teeth conversations, ashtrays, scrunched dog-ends and swirling blue smoke were part of everyday life.

My mum usually seemed to have a fag on the go. She was that regular being, a smoking, non-driving woman, and this meant trips with her that were beyond walking distance usually involved bus and train rides. Our local station was served by flare-sided red or silver District Line electric trains with art deco elements to their interiors and exteriors, and big air doors which hissed and rumbled open and closed. Dating from 1938, the red trains were lit by soft yellow tungsten bulbs, and made a particular selection of whirring, clattering and wheezing noises that seemed to confirm their venerability. The younger, but outwardly similar silver trains had harsher strip lighting and sounded less antique. I can see now that for such prosaic objects they were immensely stylish, created during the era of the streamlined Mallard A4 class mainline steam engines and the Spitfire fighter plane. Perhaps that's why I liked them.

Often my mother and I would head for a smoking carriage, where the ceilings were nicotine yellow. Here she would scrabble in her handbag for a gasper and the neat, hammerhead lighter she used to ignite it. On these trips to the West End or to visit adult friends, or my slight, severe-looking grandmother, who lived alone in a basement flat in Hammersmith, I would generally keep up a running commentary on what was going on outside the train. A very ordinary, small, unconscious egotist, assuming that what I was seeing would utterly fascinate my mother, I never noticed whether she was distracted or quiet.

In between the red and silver trains rattling in and out of Kew Gardens station came dark green British Rail electric trains on the Broad Street line. These were less venerable, but conceptually more old fashioned. Again lit by tungsten bulbs that looked to me like small glowing balloons, they had rows of oval windows and hinged doors that clunked open and closed. When one of these trains got to the end of its journey there was a slightly balletic thing about the way all the doors would open in unison as it disgorged its human cargo.

Electric trains furnished spaces I tended to share with my mother, her handbag, book, cigarettes and strangers. This norm was also true of the 65 and 27 double-decker buses that I favoured even more than the trains. They were, after all, big relations to the cars I liked.

From 1933 until the early 1960s London Transport designed its own vehicles, and the buses I first knew were also created in an engineering and aesthetic purple patch just before the Second World War. They were called 'RTs', and although their design template of engine at the front, open platform at the back, mirrored the famous Routemaster which was then replacing them elsewhere in London, they were less aggressively functional and better-looking, being slimmer with steeply curved front ends. Moving slowly amongst shoals of cars, they had a certain dignity.

As an adult, I find it quite hard to write about these man-made objects as I once saw them, because the way I interpreted the world and their place in it now seems remote, but to a small child these giant machines appeared calm, perhaps because when shut, the upper deck front windows resembled a pair of closed eyes.

You might think 'What's he on? It's a bloody bus,' but as a very small boy I found them companionable and predictable, which wasn't always the case with people.

Now I look at them as one might a beautifully realised piece of furniture, an interesting building, cutlery that feels nice in my hands because its shape and balance are just right. None of these things are high art, but at their best they can be examples of taking pleasure in doing something well. Sometimes they become brief slivers of immortality for the people who made them. So when I see an RT I see these elements in it. You might just see an odd bloke looking at an old bus.

George Murcell's Humber Hawk was an altogether more expedient proposition, but it remained one of the most distinctive cars on our street, becoming more so as time wore on and it became increasingly battle-scarred. At one point George decided to give it a makeover. Those who recall *Blue Peter* in the era of Peter Purves, John Noakes and Valerie Singleton, might remember 'sticky-back plastic.' This still exists, but was then an ineffably modern material that when peeled from grease paper backing could be attached to other surfaces, covering them in a series of brightly coloured patterns and shapes.

A version of this had been created for 1960s Mini owners, which had a wicker basket effect. To be honest, the effect was notional, but bright young things in Chelsea had it stuck to the sides of their Minis anyway. George decided that the Humber would benefit from a similar makeover, so coated its undulating flanks with acres of this stuff. The result looked a bit odd.

When the Murcells went on holiday in this car, they shared it with Cockle, the family parrot. She was a large placid African grey, who spent a lot of her time outside a rather grand cage that vaguely resembled Brighton Pavilion, happily trundling along the living room curtain rail, stopping every so often to peer at the room's human occupants and speak to them with a series of cackles.

Inside the Humber, the interior light, which had once been in the middle of the roof lining, had dropped to bits, so George used what remained of it as somewhere to hang a perch for Cockle, who would swing happily from it as the car lumbered from the London suburbs into the countryside.

These days, if cars smell of anything at all, it's a slightly clinical odour of an industrial extrusion, but George's Humber, in common with many of its contemporaries, shared its hot gassy exhalations, the vague whiff of unburned petrol and cooked motor oil. In small quantities they would find their way into a cabin already marinaded with the scent of damp carpet and ageing leather. Oddly, the end result was not unpleasant. It was part of the character of the car, and in turn was part of the character of the person that owned it.

Eventually the former's character changed for the worse, when George collected the back of a truck as a bonnet ornament. The car had a face, with two large round headlamp eyes, and a big mouth-like chrome grille. After this accidental restyling the thing's expression changed to a look of downcast surprise, which was justified, because the Humber vanished shortly afterwards, to be replaced by an even bigger Ford Zodiac, which for some reason I found so intimidating that to start with I'd only travel in it if I brought my own cushion.

It had huge front seats covered in vinyl masquerading as leather, with buttons inlaid into it. The word 'Zodiac' had a curious alchemy about it. I liked the way it sounded without knowing what it meant, and the car had another magical feature.

'It's a Zodiac automatic,' said Jamie with considerable pride.

When I discovered that this big fat bruiser of a car changed its own gears I was seized with a peculiar excitement. I didn't know a car could do this. Perhaps an automatic car could drive itself. This fed into the notion of cars, and machines in general, being alive. Once my cushion and I had been persuaded to stay in the Zodiac, I never tired of its self-changing party trick. I hadn't forgotten the Humber, and on one gliding, rumbling trip in the Zodiac George detoured up a cobbled side street and into a car breaker's yard filled with hulks of what would now be very collectable vehicles. There in a corner was the Humber, looking sad and abandoned. I felt a genuine pang for this worn-out lump of metal, and wondered if George would change his mind and rescue it, but George had moved on. He liked his big brassy Ford Zodiac automatic, and I vaguely imagined it having a quiet gloat about supplanting the battered Humber in his affections.

In fact this car, a MkIV Zodiac to those in the know, was a bit of a lemon. It was hugely roomy and powerful, with a languid 3.0 V6 engine, but was the work as much of cost accountants as engineers, and had a cut price independent rear suspension system which on paper seemed to be the acme of sophistication for a Ford, but didn't work very well, giving this lumbering car distinctly iffy handling.

Far from being hailed as a classy way of getting about for captains of industry and successful actors, the model ended up as the car of choice for provincial minicab operators, who liked the space and were happy to go round corners slowly.

The Zodiacs that survived this fate often disintegrated with rust soon afterwards, and those with Ford's metallic 'self-cleaning paint' developed scabby patches because it had a greater talent for self-detachment than self-cleaning. Hundreds of these cars finished their days as banger racers, pulverised into extinction by equally huge and rust-prone Vauxhall Crestas, smaller but tougher Austin Cambridges, and the occasional Humber Hawk, on dusty oval tracks.

Not long before things turned sour for Ford's biggest car George had bought a huge octagonal church in Tufnell Park, within rattling distance of the Broad Street Line, and was busy turning it into his dream of an all-Shakespearean theatre for London. He had replaced his Zodiac with a gaggle of Morris Minors, which sat in front of his house in various states of disrepair and attracted neighbourly opprobrium because most of the time he didn't bother to tax them. Thanks to the Yom Kippur War, when Egypt and Syria attacked Israel, sparking the first global oil crisis, petrol prices had gone through the roof. When a gallon of Four Star hit 73p, the Zodiac had to go.

The RTs were going as well, replaced by noisier, uglier Route-masters, which I didn't like at all. Their predecessors weren't the only ones making a departure from the south-west London suburbs I'd grown up in. We were leaving too. By the time I was eight my mother, whose childhood was spent in the Cumbrian countryside, had said that the pavements, traffic and constant aircraft noise that I accepted as entirely natural, and rather liked, were oppressing her. I'd felt happy and secure, floating through life in a warm fug of incomprehension and friendly mechanical sounds, so hadn't noticed her increasing unhappiness.

This manifested itself in a strong urge to get out of London, and so we sold our terraced house and moved to a pretty, low-ceilinged, wattle and daub cottage in a Bedfordshire village, close enough to town for Dad not to have to find a new job. Every weekday he climbed into the Bristol and went back to where I'd grown up and still felt at home, and it didn't take long before I began to wish that I could go with him.

# Two Wheels Good

My dad was positively decrepit when he took up motorcycling again. It worried me that a man of 45, an age of near unfathomable antiquity, would do this. Could the poor old chap cope?

This was in 1972, when we'd moved from Kew to a medium-sized village in Bedfordshire, but Dad still worked in London. He was based at what had once been movie studios in Wembley, which was a straightforward commute up the M1 motorway and a north-west London suburban trundle, but London Weekend Television was moving to a shiny high-rise building by the river on London's South Bank, minutes away from the National Theatre. This rather more prestigious address turned Dad's journey to work into a prolonged nightmare. It was also getting much more expensive.

The price of petrol had spiralled thanks to the ongoing Arab-Israeli conflict, and a realisation amongst the Arab oil-producing nations that Western European countries who'd invaded, controlled and warred over their territories not long before were at a disadvantage over oil supply, so they could charge pretty much what they wanted for crude oil. My dad's twenty-year-old Bristol 401 got through a gallon of petrol every twenty miles or so, and it wasn't exactly city-friendly.

'How long before I'm paying a pound a gallon?' he said after yet again filling the thirsty Bristol's tank with the stuff.

Its engine also needed rebuilding, so he bought a little car for commuting. He didn't go for the obvious, but instead found an obscure baby car called a BMW 700. Today BMW is best known for its bigger, posher offerings, but in the late 1950s it was almost bankrupt, reduced to making Italian Isetta bubble cars under licence. The 700 had a flat twin air-cooled BMW motorcycle engine mounted in the rear, and pretty coupé and saloon bodies styled by Italian vehicle designer Giovanni Michelotti, who also designed the Triumph Herald, which the baby BMW somewhat resembled.

It was a sufficient sales success for BMW to back away from a plan to merge with Mercedes owners Daimler-Benz, which would rather have changed the landscape of today's German car industry had it happened.

Painted white with a black bonnet, the 700 looked quite sporting, but sounded like a lawnmower and had a similarly relaxed approach to acceleration. However, the one time Dad persuaded the 700 to wind itself up to 80mph it seemed very fast indeed, with its engine hammering away behind us, its little nose rising like a dog following a scent and tugging slightly from side to side, because the weight of the engine was over the back wheels. The rear seat was hard and shapeless, the legroom limited, and I banged my head on the sloping rear screen, so when the 700 broke and Dad was unable to get the bits to fix it, going back to driving the Bristol and moaning about the expense, I was delighted. Now I see that this was a rare, interesting and rather charming little car, and I wish we still had it.

But as the 700 gathered dust, Dad's money-saving conundrum remained; he then decided to buy a motorcycle. My mother was worried that he'd fall off.

'Oh probably,' said Dad, 'but that's all right. Besides, I used to ride them in the Army.'

This had been at the tail end of the last war, when he'd been amongst massed ranks of squaddies billeted near Dartmoor. High streets would apparently clear when Dad and his fellow conscripts roared into town.

Once his commanding officer was bearded by a civilian who told him one of the men 'was in Woolworths.'

Suspecting that he'd sneaked in to buy something for his girlfriend, the CO headed for the store, which was surrounded by a small crowd. Inside he found the hapless soldier behind one of the counters, still astride his chugging steed, which had mounted the pavement, breasted the double glass doors and become wedged in the pants department.

My mother was not reassured by this tale, but it soon became obvious that the motorcycle was rather more than a vague idea.

'I'm going to buy an MZ250 Trophy,' Dad said, before explaining this was a breed of cut-price East German motorcycle rather than a handgun. It was to be the first new vehicle he'd ever owned. At £225 it was the cheapest new 250 on the market. My dad produced a single sheet of A4 paper, which functioned as the MZ's brochure, and I found it hard to share his enthusiasm for what I was seeing. There was a grainy black and white picture of an aggressively functional device with a heavy plastic shroud at the front, containing a large headlamp that looked like a searchlight and would not turn with the handlebars. Those handlebars appeared to be made from pressed tin and there was a sturdy pair of white plastic leg shields.

Ahead of these were the front forks holding a chunky wire wheel, over which was a giant metal mudguard that stuck out at an angle away from the wheel, so that it appeared to be pointing upwards. The single tail lamp looked as if it was housed in a chrome-plated bean can. The MZ appeared old-fashioned, ugly and joyless. It came from an era when novice motorcyclists could learn to ride on bikes of 250cc, and although Dad couldn't use it on a motorway until he'd taken a two-wheeled driving test, there was nothing stopping him riding the thing on the near 100 miles to and from work on minor roads.

So he ordered his MZ and had a quiet, blokey splurge, buying the appropriate boots, gloves, jacket, waterproof trousers, an open-faced crash hat with a little plastic peak, and a set of goggles, each with two flat planes of glass. When he clambered into these things he looked like a cut-price spaceman, and made a series of synthetic scrunching noises when he moved. My mother laughed as he stomped round the cottage's low ceilinged sitting room, before banging his crash-helmeted head against the hefty beam that bisected it.

'Shit!' he cried, and my mother stopped laughing.

His un-crash-hatted head had become intimate with this large chunk of timber, as at 6ft 2 he was really too tall for the house. This was not the cottage's only demerit. Its two upstairs bedrooms were interconnected and the loo was downstairs, which meant nocturnal trips to it resulted in broken sleep for the second bedroom's occupant.

The bathroom and kitchen were in a 1960s brick extension, whose walls seemed to soak up water like blotting paper. Boil a kettle in the kitchen, and the plaster appeared to sweat. Devoid of central heating, the house never became properly warm. The two older downstairs rooms had big open fires, which looked delightful but smoked when lit, and attracted freezing, howling drafts when they weren't. Raised hearths, expensive cowls and rotating chimney covers made no odds, so we spent winters frozen, kippered, or kept warm with costly electric fan heaters.

This was a far cry from when we'd first seen the house in summer, and had thought the rolling open countryside looked nice too. In winter the enormous flat fields took on a dour aspect. There was little to stop the wind from entertaining itself by collecting the reeks from a huge municipal rubbish tip located a couple of miles away and howling them towards the village when travelling in one direction, or engulfing us with the pungent odour of rotten eggs from the brick factories which peppered the landscape in the other.

London Brick was a huge employer in the locality, with works that were often built near the railway that started off in Bletchley and meandered through our village en route to a tatty, out-of-the-way station in Bedford. Once it had gone from Oxford to Cambridge, but that had been stopped in 1967. Now it was used by freight trains and tired, smelly passenger diesels. Painted dull blue, they trundled back and forth at hourly intervals. These, too, were rumoured to be threatened with extinction, and the line had an under resourced, antique feel, with stationmasters opening and closing manual gates on the roads it crossed. One station was still lit by oil lamps.

'They won't ever shut the railway,' said an old gent who'd fallen into conversation with my mother as we waited on a wind-blown platform. 'It makes money on a Saturday when everyone goes to Bedford for the bingo.' In its Oxford to Cambridge days the railway had been known as the 'Varsity' or 'Brain Line.'

Today the trains still run, but the brick factories are gone, taking their jobs and egg stench with them, and denuding Bedfordshire of its industrial heritage, but when I've been back there in recent years it's seemed lusher, busier, more prosperous, more connected to everywhere else. In 1972 our village felt cut off from the wider world. These days it's probably home to many city-bound commuters, but then Dad was just about the only one.

Most of our immediate neighbours were lovely, but the village had its own social ecosystem, whose slow-paced insularity would these days be rare, but then there was a sense that we didn't exactly fit in. We lived in the village, but we weren't truly part of it. I remember the parent of one of my primary school classmates, a bluff man in his thirties who test drove Vauxhall Vivas and Victors at the large Millbrook vehicle proving ground that backed on to the village. Whenever he spoke to me he always adopted a strange, strangulated voice. He was mimicking my 'posh' accent.

If you're old enough to remember the 1960s sinking into the '70s, the sensation might have felt a bit like a hangover after a party. This sclerotic place was where we found ourselves as the country reached for its collective Alka-Seltzer. Britain seemed to suffer a crisis of confidence, with strikes, power cuts, a taste for often brutally ugly buildings, flapping flared trousers made from scratchy nylon in depressed, shoulder shrugging beiges or hideous primary colours.

I was old enough to sense this national inertia and resigned feeling of decline without understanding it, but I was starting to notice that my mother, far from being energised by our move to the countryside, seemed more irritable and non-specifically unhappy. When Dad went off to work and I left for school, she was becalmed and isolated.

Dad was now riding his MZ, which had first arrived looking very shiny but with a mild case of gravel rash, something my dad shared with it. Having ridden it home for the first time, the pair of them had parted company on a bend, thanks to some shale that had caused the MZ's chunky front tyre to let go of the tarmac.

My mother seemed quite upset. The contrast between the brutally functional MZ and the decadent leather-lined Bristol could not have been more acute. Everything about the bike had a naked utility that was almost heroic; the Bristol was all suave elegance.

Since he was still learning to ride it, Dad wasn't able to take me out on the bike, but I became used to the ritual of his starting it and leaving for work early in the morning. We'd have breakfast, a bleary, silent affair involving warm tea and

Weetabix. He would climb into his motorcycle space suit, kiss my mother and clomp outside, breathe in the fetid air, and walk to his stolid blue and white steed.

Starting it involved inserting a crude little key into the ignition lock, turning a switch that had apparently been purloined from a 1950s valve radio, yanking on a choke lever that looked as if it belonged to a lawnmower, reaching down and turning on a small tap so that petrol would flow into the single-cylinder carburettor, swivelling out the kick lever, jerking back the twist grip accelerator, then pumping the kick start with a booted foot. After a mechanical rasp and grumble the MZ's filthy little two-stroke engine would buzz and fart into life, emitting a haze of pale blue exhaust smoke to celebrate.

When revved it made a harsh, buzzing 'Ying! Ying! Ying!' noise. At rest its tinny song was uneven and fluctuating, sounding crude because it was, but that crudity gave the Trophy a reliability that was unheard of with any of the vehicles my dad had owned before.

Soon after that I would set off for the village primary school, a modern building which lay across the road from the railway and a scrap yard, which was full of an endless stream of sad old Ford Populars and Consuls dating from the late 1950s and early '60s, their panels dented and two-tone paint schemes faded. By then I could tell approximately how old these cars were by looking at the shape of their tail lamps, or arcane details of trim. I would sometimes share the findings of this industrial archaeology with my schoolmates, who often did not respond with the enthusiasm that might have been expected. Some of them expressed their indifference quite forcefully, but I was undeterred and plugged away to change their minds. Academically and socially I had continued to sink. The 'learn when he's ready' mantra continued, but it became apparent that my getting to that point of readiness was taking a long time.

I began to be pulled out of regular lessons and put into small special classes with the school's other educational recidivists, like the boy with the constantly running nose who entertained himself during one class by lying on a desk and waggling his penis at the ceiling, and his friend, a stick-like, almost silent child with threadbare clothes and permanently dirty hands, who couldn't recite his two times table. He lived with tribes of grimy siblings, sharing a wild rubbish-strewn garden with them and his mother, who looked tired, was hugely fat and always seemed to be pegging out washing. It flapped against a dead, black Ford Consul that was even older than the ones in the scrapyard.

This being a modern school we were given the use of the latest teaching aids, including cassette tape players, into which the headmaster, a fierce character with a grey military moustache and a Mk1 Ford Escort, painted a dull red that matched its owner's face, had barked chapters of a very boring, plot-free reading book, which with headphones we were supposed to follow line by line.

'It's too fast,' I said. The headmaster's wattles reddened dangerously.

'Then you need to CONCENTRATE!' he bellowed. My intestines contracted and a fart brewed. This man was a keen exponent of caning, and I knew the consequences of letting one go. Buttocks clenched I shut up and moved my finger randomly across the page as his voice continued thundering from the headphones.

Forming lasting friendships seemed to be an issue too, and like the member-waving boy with the mucus and the sad, soiled child who couldn't recite his tables, I stuck out, and so became the subject of bullying. I sounded different, did not pick up on social signals of boredom or irritation until the people sending them out were more or less clasping me by the throat, and perhaps most sinfully of all, I was the only boy in the village, bar none, who did not like football. Somehow, this was seen as a personal slight by many of those who did, rather than the complete indifference it actually was.

They knew about George Best's latest touchline miracles, I could tell the difference between a standard Vauxhall Victor FB and the VX4/90 'performance' version just by looking at their tail lights. It was not a meeting of minds.

My dad passed his motorcycle test and took me for a ride on his MZ.

'Wrap up warm,' he said, insisting that I put on what appeared to be an absurd amount of clothing. Although it was about to become compulsory to wear a crash helmet, the law which made it so had still to be passed, but Dad still borrowed a helmet from a neighbour. This visor-less, open-faced item was half a size too big, and lolled around on my head.

'We won't go very far,' he said.

Sat on the back of the throbbing, vibrating little MZ, I was rigid with excitement and fear. Looking straight ahead all I could see was my dad's back and crash-hatted head, so scenic views would only be available from the side. He pulled in the clutch, engaged a gear with a heavy mechanical 'clonk' and we began to roll forward. Soon the buzz of the bike's engine became muted, carried away by the sound of the wind, which eddied and buffeted loudly, finding its way into my waterproof jacket and blowing it up. A child/balloon, I clung to him and moved my head from side to side as the scenery whipped by. Then we came to a right-hand bend. The bike dipped left and Dad moved to the right to compensate, leaving me a clear view because I was stuck out like a pencil.

We got round, and Dad wrenched the bike back to an upright

position and began speaking. The words were mostly whipped away by the wind.

'Mar . . . ust lean . . . da . . . gerous . . . have us off!'

'What?'

'Pardon?'

'I said "What?"!'

He stopped the bike, and said with some feeling:

'Lean with the bike, Mart! You've got to lean with it on corners or you'll have us off. If you don't move you're like a dead weight in the wrong place.'

I'd obviously given him a nasty scare, which increased my anxiety and made me rigid as a piece of hardboard, so the next few corners had to be negotiated very slowly. He stopped again.

'Look,' he said, in his special 'I'm trying not to show how irritated I'm getting' voice. 'Just do what I do. If the bike goes left I lean right, if it goes right, I lean left. See? Do that and it will be fine.'

And it was. Once I'd become used to the slightly disconcerting feeling of the MZ falling away beneath us, this was to become a piece of co-ordination I was good at, and once Dad had invested in a smaller Belstaff crash hat that fitted me properly and came with a plastic visor that kept some of the weather out, I began to ride pillion as a matter of course.

My mother was a less frequent motorcycle passenger, despite growing up in a family whose only motorised form of transport had been a motorcycle and sidecar. This did not make her enamoured with the idea of riding on the back of the flatulent sounding MZ, so it became a very infrequent happening. However, having got over the initial terror of falling off, I was beginning to like it very much.

My dad did part company from the bike on several occasions, thanks to cars pulling out in front of him, diesel slicks which gave tarmac the traction of a skating rink, and the fact that the MZ had rubbish tyres which weren't great at gripping anything.

Its soft seat was comfortable, and although its performance was genteel, it could out-accelerate most cars. I grew fairly inured to getting cold, learned how to dress in gear that kept the rain out, and discovered the trick of stuffing an old newspaper inside my shirt. On winter mornings even a tabloid has remarkable heat retention properties.

My dad and I travelled all over the place on that bike. I grew to trust him on the M1 as the throbbing little MZ slowly overhauled trucks and coaches with their huge thundering wheels, and I didn't mind that, after a long journey, I seemed to vibrate to the thrum of the MZ's engine, even when the bike was parked outside and I was sitting in the house. Eventually riding pillion was something I did exclusively with Dad, and although talking mostly wasn't an option because of the buffeting, howling wind and the bike's chainsaw buzz, this represented the sort of quality one-to-one time I was more used to spending with my mother.

'I think I'm going to buy a better motorcycle,' he said. 'The MZ's been brilliant, but it handles like a sick pig with three legs, and I could do with a bit more power on motorways.'

My mother wasn't especially enthused, and greeted the news with an indifferent shrug. Increasingly this, or irritability, had become her reaction to a lot of things.

My dad and I were quite sad to see the faithful, lumpen MZ depart. 'All I've had to do to that bike was change a light bulb,' he said, as we surveyed its replacement, a Yamaha RD350, which looked sleeker and had slim chrome mudguards and deep red-tinged purple metallic paint. Its two-stroke engine still sounded harsh and high pitched, but with a lot more power and two cylinders rather than one, it was a great deal quicker. The MZ had been entirely functional, but the Yamaha was exciting.

Early 1970s Japanese motorcycles were known for having awful tyres, but Dad, being Dad, wanted to get his money's worth from the ones fitted to the Yamaha and didn't immediately swap them for superior rubberware. He was separated from it on several occasions as a result, without either party suffering serious injury. He eventually bought some better tyres.

'How would you like to come to Italy with me on the bike?' he said soon afterwards. 'Some friends from work who have motorcycles are going there on a camping holiday, and they've said we could go too.'

I'd never been abroad, and the idea seemed exciting. My mother did not share my enthusiasm, fearing the consequences of an accident, but increasingly she seemed to be gripped by serial anxieties or inertia, so this wasn't a surprise. She was also struggling to get me to do what she wanted, often giving up, so when I wasn't socially abrading and chafing at school, I frequently ran wild.

So my dad and I went to Italy, leaving the fetid air, dank empty fields, and my unhappy mother, and travelled with a short, wiry man in his thirties called Tony, who was a dispatch rider at my father's work, and Frances, Tony's blonde, hearty girlfriend, who also rode a bike. Both seemed incredibly sophisticated to me, and I was particularly impressed by Tony's habit of cheerfully arguing with my dad about obscure bits of motorcycle technology.

'It's got a positive earth,' he said to my dad, as they discussed his bike's electrics.

'That's daft. You can't have a positive earth.'

'You can with that bike.'

'Really, how?'

'It's a Yamaha.'

We crossed France in three days, riding for hour after hour through sunshine and storms, thundering along straight tree-lined avenues. I'd never been colder, or more tired, but the trip was a blast.

When we reached the French-Italian border, Dad had strapped us together with a large belt in case I went to sleep and fell off, but at the foot of Alps the cold, clean air woke me. Unsmiling, peaked capped men sat in little booths laboriously checking our passports. I saw some abandoned cars and wandered over to take a closer look at them, passing some very armed, very surprised border guards.

'It nearly gave me a heart attack,' said Dad.

After that we were back on the bikes. Engines labouring, we climbed endlessly into the Alps along narrow snaking roads. Their intestinal wriggling scarred the huge and beautiful mountains, whose scale was new to me. I tensed as we negotiated tight bends next to sheer drops, and at one point looked down and saw, about fifty feet below, the smashed, upturned remains of a large articulated truck.

In the company of crawling Fiat 500s and big camions we reached the summit and started down, weaving through roads with squiggling switchbacks that resembled pencil scribbles. It took hours and it was fabulous.

When we reached our first big Italian town I was half asleep. As we rounded a bend I was vaguely aware of a large green Fiat truck coming towards us, partially on our side of the road, and Dad moving into the kerb. Then the world tipped violently and went grey. I heard a woman screaming.

The greyness was eventually infiltrated by the sound of foot-steps clack-clacking on a hard stone floor. Round shapes began to appear above my head. Eventually these became the faces of a doctor and a porter, who was pushing me along a hospital corridor on a trolley. I called my dad's name and heard nothing, waited then called again.

'Mart,' said a familiar voice.

Stupidly, I asked what had happened.

'We came off the bike.'

They patched us up. I had a gash above my right eye that was stitched together without anaesthetic. I'd never felt such pain. My chin throbbed and would develop a huge dark blue bruise. I had a sprained ankle and wrist. My dad suffered a variety of cuts and abrasions, four cracked and one broken rib, which we later discovered had punctured one of his lungs.

The truck driver was drunk and had wandered into our path. As my father pulled into the kerb to avoid the lorry, his front wheel went into a deep drain that was missing its cover, and the bike bucked us off. I have no memory of sliding along the road towards the still moving lorry, but was told that we'd each struck and bounced off its trailer's moving wheels.

They were kind to us at the hospital, but not being able to speak Italian made the experience isolating and frightening, and eventually extraordinarily tedious. After a week some students, who'd heard about the accident and could speak English, offered to take me on a tour of the town and the surrounding countryside. I was levered into an orange Fiat 500 and we puttered around elegant, dusty streets and up into the hills, to see a shrine overlooked by a giant figure of the Virgin Mary.

Both my dad and I were pumped full of medication using a huge syringe with a glass body. It looked like a bad theatre prop, and in an era before AIDS, was used on every patient in our ward, its ever-blunter needle cleaned in some blue liquid before being plunged into another backside. It was hideous and painful, and when, ten days later, we were discharged and hobbled back to Britain, Dad examined his buttocks in a mirror and counted 101 pinpricks.

We did not come back unaccompanied. One of the students caught a pair of tiny goldfish in a local lake and presented them to me. They lived in a large jar by my bedside, then emigrated to Britain in a water-filled plastic carrier bag. The customs officers at Heathrow were highly amused and let us through.

In due course my dad, myself, and the Yamaha were all mended. I went back to school, where my now yellowing bruise caused much barbed hilarity.

It was my mother who was in need of serious care, as soon afterward she finally sank into a deep, debilitating depression. The weeks leading up to it were laced with an almost electric tension, which was finally broken when I returned from school to find my dad waiting for me.

'Your mum's in hospital,' he said.

He made some tea, and we sat in the cold little sitting room. Eventually I said:

'So you're going to look after me?'

'I have to go to work,' he said. 'Sometimes I have to work late. I won't be at home enough to do that.'

I assured him that, having recently turned nine, I could look after myself. When my mother had been particularly washed-out I'd started to cook, usually producing things involving toast, baked beans, scrambled eggs and burned saucepans. I'd cope.

'I can't leave you on your own,' he said. 'Aunt Pat and Uncle Mick are going to let you stay with them for a bit.'

I felt stunned. I liked Aunt Pat and Uncle Mick, but I wanted to be with my parents and stay in my own home, not live in someone else's house hundreds of miles away.

'We'll have supper then we'll pack,' he said. 'You're going tomorrow.'

# North of Watford

I travelled to Lancashire on an express train, a solo nine-year-old evacuee with a suitcase, expelled from the familiar by a small but all-enveloping domestic crisis.

The carriage was modern, lit by hard fluorescent tubes, and notionally air-conditioned, so you couldn't open the windows. This made it stuffy and hot, and my head began to hurt as we plunged northwards, wheels emitting the harsh metallic noise particular to fast trains, which almost sounds like someone constantly, and noisily, breathing out on a cold winter's morning. When we slowed or pulled in to unfamiliar stations there was an acrid smell of hot brakes.

I was still small enough to be thrown about by the movement of the train on the odd occasions that I made for one of the mildly rancid, graffiti-enhanced toilets. This caused me to totter drunkenly left and right, small hands reaching and grabbing plastic seat frames. The top of my head was level with them and their occupants. Middle-aged men, some wearing hats, younger men with big hair and sideburns, old women with white cotton-wool perms and fuzzy knitted tops coloured 'stick of seaside rock' pink or blue. I saw faces hidden behind National Health Service glasses, with their thick black and brown frames and TV screen lenses. Flared brown and beige trousers hid big-heeled shoes; collars were broad. This, after all, was 1973.

I didn't speak to anybody because as my father saw me off, he told me for the umpteenth time I wasn't to. Not that I had much to say. Eventually the guard in a dark blue uniform ambled up the aisle. Punching my ticket with what looked like a strange nail clipper he asked if I was on my own.

'Know where you're going?' he said.

'Preston.'

'Well,' he said. 'I'll be back to tell you when we're about to get there.'

Under different circumstances the journey would have been exciting, but I was numb to my surroundings, and saw the outside world not as interesting, but alien. I thought about getting off the train and catching one back, finding a way to get into the house, and living there in secret. After all, my dad had said he was staying in London with my grandmother, and the neighbours were looking after the cat and dog, but I didn't dare.

Today the idea of a small child travelling alone by train would give most parents hives, but in 1973 it didn't seem that odd. Thanks to Hitler, many adults of my parents' generation had experienced childhoods punctuated with sudden, parent-free train journeys during wartime evacuations. Also, in the early 1970s children were often left to their own devices in ways that would now result in a visit from social services.

When I got off the train at Preston I was unmolested, thirsty, and my head still ached. I lugged my suitcase out from the Victorian arch that covered the platforms and into the concourse where I was told Aunt Sheila would be waiting.

She and Aunt Pat looked very alike. Small, brisk, middle-aged women with sensible permed hair, they both had a confident, adult authority that I didn't always see in my mother, and which, because I enjoyed getting my own way, I didn't entirely like.

Aunt Sheila drove a white Hillman Avenger. What it was avenging nobody knew, but it was brand new, which made it interesting to me. It was a modern car with black vinyl seats bereft of headrests, an expanse of plastic dashboard, and a rotary switch the size of a soup tin that turned the lights on sprouting from the side of the steering column.

The Avenger's modernity was confirmed by these, its little square headlights and the novelty value of it having reversing lights, which struck me as highly modern. Another sophistication was its inertia-reel front seatbelts, which had simple-to-operate clips and reels so that they hung, out of the way, on the door pillars when not in use.

These contrasted with most of the cars I knew which were either so old that they weren't fitted with belts at all, or had the fiddly static type, which were fixed bits of webbing that went round your middle and over your shoulder, with a clasp like an airline belt that clipped into another clasp attached to yet another piece of webbing, that could be adjusted through it and was bolted onto the transmission tunnel on either side of the handbrake. These items would tie themselves in knots or refuse to tighten or undo, the clips would jam or fail to engage, and I'd often hear grown-ups saying: 'I know we should wear them, but . . .'

Aunt Sheila told me to use the seatbelt, something I'd never done before, and it felt oddly restricting. Of course ignoring belts wasn't against the law, and there was an ongoing angry debate about whether making their use compulsory was an infringement of civil liberties.

There were public information films involving gruesome images of people smashing through windscreens, the most effective of which was fronted by Jimmy Savile, at the time a cheeky, child-friendly denizen of popular 1970s primetime television. In one vignette, Savile was pictured with a cardboard egg box and a tin money box, both containing eggs. As he talked about the dangers of not wearing seatbelts he shook them, with the predictable consequence that the moneybox egg was pulped. This tableau was intercut with shots of crash test dummies flying through windscreens and a red Hillman Minx rolling over, before cutting away to Savile climbing into an identical car, snapping on a belt and saying 'Clunk-click, every trip.'

This became another playground catchphrase, which in hindsight is more than creepy. For some reason, the fact that decades later the film is actually still very good, is too.

Feeling the Avenger's seatbelt pressing against my shoulder and wishing I could take it off, I asked Aunt Sheila where I'd be going to school.

'Where your Aunt Pat teaches,' she said.

Half an hour later we pulled up at her house. This was no longer the 1930s semi that had been our base during the earlier breakdown-infused holidays. Uncle Mick had wanted to live in somewhere properly rural, and his family had moved to a bungalow with a large garden, not far from the Trough of Bowland with its fells and forests. It was quite wild, rather beautiful and most of the immediate neighbours were cows or sheep. It was a complete culture shock.

Aunt Pat drove a small faded red Bedford HA van. Bought for £60, it dated from 1965 and had rust patches at the tops of its front wings above its round, staring headlamps. They looked like small brown oxidised eyebrows. Before its arrival she'd had to share Uncle Mick's Vauxhall Victor 101 Super, which had succeeded the Austin Cambridge after its floor rotted out. The Victor was a big sloppy saloon with marshmallow seats and marshmallow handling. It also had a large fence-post-shaped indentation in the middle of the bonnet, the legacy of swerving to avoid a wandering sheep, when Mick, rather than the sheep, was heading for a camping holiday in the Cumbrian seaside resort of St. Bees. In common with many Vauxhalls of the period, the Victor was going rusty, so wasn't worth repairing, and once the insurance money had come through, Uncle Mick planned to replace it with a Mini.

Uncle Mick himself was something in insurance. Every weekday he drove the Vauxhall Victor into Preston. Then Aunt Pat, for whom car-free rural isolation was a mixed blessing until she bought her little van, had to wait for the school minibus. So the van was liberation on wheels. I liked it immensely, because in its rackety way, the Bedford was a character in its own right.

The double rear doors made comedy creaking noises whenever they were opened or closed. Unencumbered with soundproofing, the Bedford's little box body bonged and twanged as its small stiffly sprung wheels found ruts and potholes while they propelled it down steeply cambered lanes. Someone had fashioned a back seat from two hinged sections of plywood, to which vinyl covered rectangular cushions had been attached. This unyielding perch had been augmented with old domestic cushions. The van had a solid metal dashboard from which a small selection of knobs and switches protruded, and in which was the Bedford's one luxury, an AM push-button radio.

Through the medium of a coat hanger aerial and a huge loudspeaker that lived in a wooden box in the back of the van, Aunt Pat listened to Radio 4, and occasionally Judith got to hear Radio 1. Mornings were generally given over to John Timpson and Brian Redhead being avuncular on the Today Programme, but occasionally Ed 'Stewpot' Stewart would intrude and the van would be filled with the sound of twanging tin panels, parping engine and the numbskull Party 7 stomp of Slade or the sly heterosexual camp of T. Rex. This contrasted strongly with what I was used to at home, where my parents were fans of Radio 3. They generally wrote off pop music as 'rubbish,' so I assumed that it was, and said so to Aunt Pat and Judith, although secretly I thought that Chuck Berry's genitalia-fixated 'My Ding-a-Ling' was a work of subversive comic genius. Judith's irritation at this nine-year-old's take on music criticism came as a surprise.

'You really ought to wear a safety belt' said my aunt as we piled into the van and prepared to head for school, the day after her sister had deposited me into her life.

As I wrestled with the knotted static belt she hauled out the choke knob, cranked the ignition key, a couple of warning lights flickered, the engine churned and the van puttered and throbbed into life. We were some way into the journey and I was still tugging and heaving at the useless seatbelt when my aunt told me 'not to worry about it now.'

Subsequent early morning journeys were often a bit last minute, with my harassed aunt dumping bags filled with marking and exercise books in to the back of the van and telling me to 'get a move on please, Martin.'

She often fortified the drive to school with a cigarette, so the journey was usually pungent with a combination of Benson & Hedges and farming, whose not unpleasant odours of sheep and cow shit and the sweet treacle-like pong of silage (a liquid cattle feed) were preferable to the rubbish dump and brick factory stinks of where I'd come from. The countryside seemed greener and lusher too, and because in this part of the world livestock rather than crop farming dominated, there was more to see. However, it wasn't home, so its picture postcard quality rather passed me by.

Aunt Pat rowed her little van along by its gearstick, building up speed in a relentless way as we thundered along narrow lanes before shuddering to a halt at empty junctions. Then it would be banged into gear and the whole process started again. I would soon grow used to details and little landmarks of that journey. The farmhouse with a small bedroom window filled with a child's model of a rocking horse, the large dark stone Edwardian villa with the rusty metal fence and big monkey puzzle tree, which seemed oddly out of place in the Lancashire countryside. We'd pass a dairy filled with gleaming chrome vats, turn right and along a lane with high hedges past a semi-derelict garage with ancient petrol pumps, next to which was a field filled with decaying old lorries, rotting Cortinas and Austin A30s. Then we'd plunge down an undulating incline, where Aunt Pat might persuade the van to hit 50mph, gathering a lolloping momentum so that it wouldn't labour up the subsequent slope. We'd flash past The Dorchester, a farmer's pub in which Uncle Mick communed with his mates most nights of the week, then on to the school where the van would finally rattle to a halt.

That journey always had a slight frisson to it, brought about by my aunt usually setting off later than she'd planned, the fact that it felt fast even though it wasn't, and the sense that her van might expire at any moment. The school was a classic Victorian primary. Stone, single-storey with three classrooms and a small assembly area divided by wooden partitions that could once have been folded away but never were, high rectangular windows that allowed light in but removed the distraction of being able to see out of them. Next to it was the headmaster's house and behind it the playground, which until the innovation of oil-fired central heating had featured a pile of coal in one corner for the school boiler.

'You're in the headmaster's class,' said my aunt. I didn't like the sound of this. Headmasters were shouty authority figures, school was where I generally failed to do stuff, and I had visions of the latter leading to the former. As for actually learning, the idea that I could do this never crossed my mind.

'And who are you?' said the headmaster. Actually, he said 'and who are yoo?' in a rolling, softly rumbling voice which I later discovered was the result of his coming from a place called Barnsley. Some way into his forties, with jet-black, almost quiffed hair, which I suspect might have been oiled, combed back from a high forehead, this man had big fleshy lips and big thick-lensed National Health Service glasses, behind which a pair of shrewd eyes glittered with an appraising, naughty intelligence. The end result was both stern and subversive.

'Pleased to meet you, Martin. My name is Mr Birdsall, but you can call me "Sir,"' said this charismatic but alarming vision. He spoke in a strangely matey tone, as if he'd decided we were friends, that 'Sir' was his first name, and I was welcome to use it.

'Your aunt tells me you're having a bit of trouble with your reading.'

'I can't read or write,' I said flatly.

'Hmmm,' said 'Sir,' whom I later discovered was actually called Trevor. 'And why do you suppose that is?'

'I'm left-handed.'

'Sir' looked deadly serious, but sounded amused.

'So am I, and I can read and write,' he said. 'So you'll just have to get on and learn how to as well, won't you?'

Living with Aunt Pat, Uncle Mick and Judith followed rhythms of family life that would be familiar to many people who grew up from the 1940s onwards. Children weren't treated as little adults, adults were treated with respect or there would be trouble. As a child, I quickly discovered that those adults had exterior lives from me, which for my aunt and uncle involved the church, the pub, the Women's Institute, *Coronation Street* on the TV, *The Archers* on the radio, and a busy, happy social network.

Their eldest son Stephen had grown into a big-haired and extravagantly bearded Manchester University student, a figure of detached, louche worldliness, whose appearance when he came to visit drew unspoken disapproval from his dad, who was a vision of short back and sides neatness.

Uncle Mick had the cleanest shoes I'd ever seen, and his weekends always involved the ritual of polishing them. This began when he sat in his chair by the cream-tiled open fireplace, watching *World of Sport* on the very modern Granada Rentals colour television. As the pantomime villains and heroes of professional wrestling did choreographed battle, thudding about while their audience happily yelled abuse, Mick would open a tin of Cherry shoe polish on the hearth, make newspaper spills, light them in the fire and use these to briefly ignite the polish. After a few seconds he'd blow out the flames and apply the resultant dark liquid to his immaculate, unwrinkled work shoes, buffing them to a satisfying sheen.

Life, on the surface at least, was governed by these shared and private routines, and I found this both restrictive and reassuring. They were private and particular to this family and inevitably I was a somewhat awkward fit into their world.

Having said goodbye to an older brother, instead of getting her parents to herself, Judith suddenly had to share them with a big-mouthed little brother substitute. Uncle Mick came from Kendal in Cumbria, and was proud of his roots; his worldview was that 'all foreigners start south of Wigan,' so I was very foreign indeed. I also suspect that he found my parents flighty and trying, and on a personal level wasn't particularly enamoured with me, but he still made an open-ended commitment that allowed me into his home. Later he would put up with sharing it with Sarah, our dog, a flock of chickens that I was allowed to acquire, and on a number of occasions my still-depressed mother.

With his friends he could be warm and funny, though I often found him severe, remote and unyielding. But under the granite exterior was a person who was hugely generous to me. As for my aunt, she took me on because she thought it was the right thing to do. At that point in time I wasn't the least bit grateful to any of them.

'Sir' drove a bright yellow Mk3 Ford Cortina. This was a flashy saloon with a Coke bottle kick to its waistline, that contrasted with the boxy scruffiness of Aunt Pat's van and the rather brutal functionality of the infant teacher's Morris 1800, known to car critics of the time as the 'Land Crab' because of its 'almost as wide as it's long' looks. Designed by Sir Alec Issigonis, the man who'd created the Mini and the Morris Minor, it was hugely spacious but was the style-free product of a ruthless engineering logic that set it apart from the Cortina. If the Ford was the car equivalent of an Angel Delight dessert, the Morris was a sort of cabbage on wheels.

Sir's Cortina had replaced a Morris Marina, which combined simplicity with mediocrity and terminal unreliability, because it was the product of British Leyland, the woebegone bastard child of the mass merging of British carmakers from Austin to Jaguar in 1968. It produced things like the Marina and Austin Allegro, with its dumpy body and comedy 'quartic' square steering wheel, and the Triumph Stag and Range Rover. The last two were brilliantly conceived, potential world-beaters that were being badly screwed together by fractious, unhappy workers, so were just as prone to breaking down as the also-ran Marinas and Allegros.

Buyers were losing patience, at the cheaper end of the market defecting to strange-looking Japanese Datsun Cherrys and Toyota Corollas. These were compact studies in chintz and vulgarity, but were good value and came with tinted glass, headrests, radios and complete mechanical reliability.

Jaguar, Rover and Triumph devotees were beginning to desert their favourite cars in favour of more reliable Volvos and BMWs. This was seen as traitorous and unpatriotic by many, and there were vociferous calls to ban or limit Japanese imports to give British car makers in general, and British Leyland in particular, breathing space. At least Sir's Cortina was still a British-made car, but the reason he'd bought it was part of a wider industrial malaise that in the part of rural Lancashire where I'd ended up expressed itself in song.

During a music lesson where we all had to sing call and response folksongs, Sir substituted the verse of one for something he'd written, so that we all belted out:

'You can't get far in a Marina car,'

'A Marina car won't get that far.'

Within months I was getting somewhere academically because the little school still taught the basics by rote, which doesn't suit everybody, but worked for me.

I was a child who learned by doing things, and those things had to be presented to me very specifically, and practised again and again. This sounds boring, but wasn't once I started to master them and could see improvements when I did. I'd been ready to learn from the beginning, but needed the tools to do so, and needed to be made to use them.

This meant that I started shuttling between Sir's 'top class' and my aunt's, which catered for children a year or so younger than me. Here we chanted our times tables and practised letter formations, using lined exercise books and grey and black plastic ballpoint pens that looked a bit like anorexic airships. I grew to enjoy the swinging rhythmic movement of writing the letters in lower case, and the more I did this, the less abstract and wobbly they became.

We'd chant our times tables, or repeat mnemonics like 'a verb is a doing word' or 'a noun is the name of a person, place or thing' in sing-song unison. In the classroom Aunt Pat stopped being my mother's sister and became 'Mrs Nelson.' That's what everyone else in the class called her, so I did too, and I was treated in exactly the same way as my peers. Transformed into Mrs Nelson, I can see now that Aunt Pat was a very good teacher. She had a quiet authority and a sympathetic professional detachment, but did not give anyone the option of not learning.

Back in the 'top class,' where Sir had the ability to make us laugh one minute and quake the next, the process continued. He was a benign show-off. Always loud, always moving about, he enjoyed holding court, loved an audience and had the self-confidence of someone who is good at their job and knows it. There was also a sense that he liked you, even when you got things wrong. You wanted to please him, even if you didn't quite know why.

He had a unique way of expressing his displeasure, using gradations of insults that ran from 'berk!' to 'great berk!' 'pillock!' and 'great pillock!' And for special levels of ineptitude, 'constipated pillock!'

He could be foul tempered, wasn't above prolonged verbal bullying, and could make the class sit in total silence that he would punctuate with roaring fury if we'd collectively failed to meet his expectations. I found these outbursts utterly terrifying, and a regular Friday morning spelling test became the source of gut-churning anxiety. Sir would bark out words for us to write down, sometimes deciding that they were so simple that anyone who got any of them wrong would be 'rulered.' This nasty ritual involved putting your hand up after you'd failed, and walking to the front of the class holding it palm upward so that Sir could wallop it with a wooden ruler. Every Friday my guts would churn themselves into a bubbling knot of anxiety, and that of course made me want to fart.

When, inevitably, I misspelled a word and had to take the walk of shame, I vibrated with terror, weaving past rows of ancient scratched wooden desks with their dusty inkwells, hinged lids and silent occupants. I took little steps for fear of a noisy flatulent outburst, then stood, a trembling, buttock-clenched picture of misery, and held up my hand.

'Thwack!'

My colon twitched, my abdomen ached, my hand, which now bore a red diagonal mark, stung and then felt numb. It took a supreme effort of concentration, but I kept everything in.

'You can sit down now,' said a voice. It was Sir.

Small steps back to the desk. I sat, legs crossed, so tense that my bollocks hurt. Ten minutes later we'd moved on to another subject, and under the cover of the noise of banging desks, chatter and scraping chairs, one small boy, staring straight ahead, made a prolonged Whoopee Cushion noise.

Despite these outbursts, we wanted this man to like us and take pleasure in our success, and there was a feeling that even when he was bellowing that you were 'A GREAT CONSTIPAPTED PILLOCK!' he was somehow on your side. Also, when he told you that you could do something, you tended not to disagree.

One break time Sir was in the classroom marking books. Seeing me in the corridor he called me in. 'Read this,' he said, handing me a storybook.

'I don't think I can.'

'Just try,' said Sir, who went back to his desk and carried on marking.

The book was an old blue hardback, containing a short, cod-Swallows and Amazons adventure story, with each page containing three or four paragraphs of text, and line drawings of weirdly neat, 1950s schoolboys engaged in daring-do.

The plot rattled along, I'd read three pages and really wanted to know what happened next when I stopped. It felt as if something blurred had suddenly come into sharp focus. I was reading, not in the tortuous 'sounding out words' sense, but following a narrative.

I put up my hand.

'What is it, Martin?'

'I can read this.'

Sir did not look up from his desk as he continued to mark the pile of exercise books, adding a flurry of red ticks and crosses into their margins.

'That's right,' he said. 'We told you you could.'

# Into Focus

Three people taught me to read. Sir, my aunt and my dad, who every month or so would make the 400-mile round trip from London to see me.

He'd arrive on a Friday evening, either on his Yamaha RD350 motorcycle, when he'd look tousled and tired, or at the wheel of a dark blue Triumph Herald estate he'd bought from a friend. He'd taken the Bristol to bits before my mother had become ill, so it and the BMW 700 were left to rot at the empty Bedfordshire house.

'The Herald's got a Triumph Spitfire engine,' he'd told me on the phone. I imagined a car that was secretly massively powerful and fast, but this boxy vehicle was actually just a little quicker off the mark than normal and quite a lot noisier, in part because it had been fitted with a home-made exhaust fashioned from off-cuts of other exhausts and clamped together. It sagged in the middle and would sometimes scrape along the ground when the car negotiated bumps. The Herald also had a noisy differential that sounded like a bandsaw, so long journeys in it were quite tiring. However, by comparison with what had gone before it was spectacularly reliable, so my dad's long trips northwards no longer involved mechanical Russian roulette.

Before my reading book epiphany I'd begun reading a comic called *Buster & Jet*, which featured a flat-hatted schoolboy character called, inevitably, Buster, who'd started life as Andy Capp's son, but had taken on a life of his own.

I'd look at the pictures in the strips, but when Dad arrived he would, with extreme patience, read them with me, splitting the words into syllables, juddering forward as we picked our way with painful slowness through these slapstick and adventure story narratives. If we got through a strip together, he'd read the next one to me.

By now Uncle Mick's Vauxhall Victor had been carted off to the breakers, and he'd bought a shiny dark blue second-hand Mini, which had sliding windows in the front doors, little tail lamps shaped like toddler's shoes and the original down-in-the-mouth chrome grille. Its general cleanliness contrasted with the lived in, travel-stained vista presented by my dad's Triumph Herald.

He and this car seemed to emerge from over the horizon behind which my own private world had sunk, and which I missed with a fixed, childish, dully aching passion. The stuff Dad kept in that car, the feel of the vinyl seats, the whirr of the heater fan, even the way the thing smelt inside, represented a microclimate of home. It made me enormously happy at the start of his visits, and very sad when he left. This impregnable misery wasn't even dented by the kindness I was shown by my aunt's family, and I often kicked ungraciously at being subsumed into their way of life, because this indicated that I wasn't going back to mine.

Eventually my mother emerged over the horizon too, appearing for the first of a series of extended visits. She arrived in the Triumph Herald with my dad and a cage containing a large green parrot called Rose. Bought as a palliative for the misery my mother almost seemed to sweat, this psychotic bird was filled with screeching, knuckle-cracking rage, and was hell to be around.

So, on occasions, was my mother. Prolonged exposure to her distress was painful and exhausting, the depression manifesting itself in barbed, often strange remarks. I also found it hard to negotiate my way through the complex dynamic of being with a parent who was no longer in charge of me, and other adults who were. It must have been a great deal harder for them, in part because unwillingly and resentfully, my mother had assumed the role of a dependent middle-aged child for my poor aunt and uncle to care for too, but they did this without strangling her, me, or that fucking parrot.

My mother and I loved each other, and it must have pained her hugely to see her sister parenting me, but with an unconscious, childish survival instinct I had began to detach myself from my mother's depression. This meant an increasing detachment from her, and spending time when I wasn't at school with my chickens, a motley flock that crapped on Uncle Mick's neat lawn and trashed my aunt's veg patch. On other occasions I would borrow Judith's bicycle and cycle into the lush countryside. In the summer the lanes' hot tarmac would bubble, and the hedgerows seemed to be full of birds and insects.

On one such occasion, I was cycling when I heard the sound of a small engine being madly revved, and came to a farmhouse outside which a group of teenage boys was grouped round an ancient moped. One of them began pedalling it up the road, yanking on the twist grip. With a rattling sputter the moped's tired little engine burst into life and belched blue oily smoke. Its rider leered triumphantly as his decrepit steed popped and farted past me. He turned inexpertly then thundered back in the other direction.

I watched this obviously illegal tableau with mixed feelings of ludicrous, pompous disapproval and a very strong urge to have a go as well. Eventually one of the boys noticed me hovering on the road and asked who I was.

'You live with Mr and Mrs Nelson then?' he said. 'Mrs Nelson taught me, now my sister's in her class.'

For some reason this conferred on me the status of being a known quantity. I asked about the moped.

'It's an NSU,' said the boy. 'It's very old.'

'It's very bloody knackered too,' said one of his friends. This led to a chorus of adolescent guffawing. I looked wistfully at the moped.

'Want to ride it?'

There was a farm building with a concrete yard immediately behind where we were talking, and it was decided that this would be a safer place for me to try the bike than the road.

Somebody managed to coax it into life and I climbed aboard, feeling this sickly old machine vibrate beneath me. Almost speechless with excitement I gingerly hauled back the throttle and began trundling forward, my feet sliding on the concrete.

A wall loomed up, I rolled the twist grip shut and tried to brake. The moped, travelling at a brisk walking pace, failed to slow down.

'Brakes don't work,' said somebody helpfully as I thudded into the wall. The front tyre compressed, the back wheel rose into the air and bounced down again, stalling the engine, but for some strange reason I didn't fall off, which given I wasn't wearing any protective gear was just as well. I'd travelled all of 30 feet, but this was the first time I'd been in charge of something with an engine, and the experience was indescribably exciting.

From this point I became an occasional acolyte of this group, who didn't seem to object to my tagging along with them. Two were brothers whose parents owned the farm. Their grandparents, who'd run it before them, had retired to a neat house almost opposite where I was living. When I began spending time on the farm itself nobody seemed to object. Soon I was doing odd jobs, probably getting in the way more than actually helping, at least to start with, but everyone involved was kind and accommodating. I helped dip sheep, in the process being pulled over by one and not letting go, so that it dragged me like a human toboggan through the shit. This was the cause of much blokey hilarity at the farm and deep irritation on the part of my aunt when I appeared, stinking and half covered in sheep ordure.

I rode on tractors, fed pigs, watched cows give birth, and eventually spent part of my weekends collecting battery eggs, which netted me 50 pence a day. I also wandered near open slurry pits and heavy machinery in a way that would now be seen as dangerous in the extreme – potentially it was, but in the mid 1970s many children on farms experienced similar things. This wasn't negligence, just normal life, and I loved it.

My mother and her wall-eyed parrot shuttled back and forth between my two aunts' houses. She was often walled up behind shifting anxieties and paranoia, which separated us very nearly as effectively as the physical distance had before she'd arrived. When it was announced that she was 'going home for a bit,' I felt relieved, and guilty for feeling relieved. This was during a school holiday, and, briefly, I would be coming too, for a short break with my grandmother in London. I nearly wet myself with excitement. Presumably my unofficial adopted family sighed inwardly at the prospect of getting their lives back for a bit.

On the journey south I bounced around in the back of the Herald estate looking at my silent parents as they sat in the front of the car, serenaded by the exhaust occasionally connecting with the tarmac, the moaning, knackered differential and Rose, whose cage had been placed directly behind my head on the luggage deck. Despite this being covered with a blanket, she kept up a constant venomous screeching all the way home.

My mother was deposited, sullen and tired, at the dark, cold

Bedfordshire cottage, and I visited the Bristol and BMW 700 at the bottom of the garden. Both were moribund and surrounded by long grass. I peered into the Bristol, at the boxes filled with tappets, valves and other bits of its mechanical lights, saw its familiar wooden dash and array of dials and round buttons. One day I would own a car like this, I thought, despite the car feeling cold and dead. I felt a pang of nostalgia for the past, of which this car had been a happy part. Neither showed any signs of making a return.

Although nothing was said, I sensed that my parents' lives were diverging as physical separation pulled apart the fibres that had bound our family together. Increasingly my father stayed in London. My mother remained pinioned by illness as she rallied and crumpled, shuttling between hospitals, halfway houses and the cottage, where her world contracted and slowed to an anxious trickle.

By the middle of 1975 I was still in Lancashire, looking after my chickens, spending some of the weekend working at the farm, and continuing to catch up with my peers at school, where Sir carried on inspiring and terrorising depending on his mood. During a period when he was laid low for several days by a bug, his wife took the class, which became louder and less productive. After a few days of this we arrived to find that Sir had written a poem, which was pinned to a wall by his desk.

> As I lie here a thinking,
> A sweating and a stinking,
> I'm wondering what you're doing over there.
> 'Cos your work so far's been careless,
> When I've marked it I've gone hairless,
> And I don't wish to be bald all my life.

So I'll give you all this warning,
Take care from this morning,
Or I'll come over and thump you with me wife.

Wiv luv from Sir.

We took the hint.

My time at the school was coming to a close, which academically was a pity, because as my aunt said later, another year there would have really cemented the things I was learning, often with a rush of pleasure.

I was no longer functionally illiterate and innumerate. Having endlessly repeated times tables ('one six is six, two sixes are twelve, three sixes are eighteen,' and so on) I was still rotten at maths, but could at least do it, and to this day use those lumpen mnemonics to add and subtract stuff. Without extreme concentration my handwriting quickly degenerated, but all the letters pointed the right way, and mostly I could put punctuation marks in the right places. Before I'd just spattered these things round the page without the faintest idea where they should go.

I still engendered near furnace levels of rage from Sir when stuff that I'd been taught and could easily manage for weeks simply vanished from my brain, but at least it was going in. I could also read very well, and would bore on endlessly about having one of the highest reading ages in the class.

By now those reading skills were being applied to my favourite subject. This started with a well-thumbed schoolbook of cars, filled with brightly coloured renderings of late 1940s models like the Armstrong Siddeley Hurricane convertible, with its sphinx grille mascot and Wilson pre-selector gearbox. I wondered what a sphinx was, looked in a dictionary and found out, then asked my father on one of his exhausting weekend visits about pre-selector gearboxes, and how they worked.

I read this little book several times, along the way finding that it had renderings of a Jowett Javelin, not as a tired old banger, but as a shiny thing rushing down a country lane, piloted by a square-jawed bloke in a trilby hat. The text told me a bit about what made the car different. There was also a Bristol 401, looking raffish and standing next to a huge airliner with propellers. This was called the Bristol Brabazon, which Uncle Mick told me had been killed off by the first jet airliners.

I was interested in new cars too. Models like the Vauxhall Chevette, a small, shovel-nosed shopping trolley car with the innovation of a hatchback body. Posher versions had exotic features including cloth inserts in their seats, with garish tartan patterns. The Mk2 Ford Escort made the BBC Nine O'Clock News, so I wanted to find out about that. Finally there was the unfeasibly modern 18/22 Series saloon. This was British Leyland's replacement for the old Landcrab 1800 and similarly huge inside, but had a tapering, wedge-shaped body, with sharp edges and straight lines, that was as modern as Preston bus station. Pointlessly, this car was sold as an Austin, a Morris and a Wolseley, which maintained the incongruity of a little 1930s-style illuminated oval Wolseley badge in the middle of its hunkered-down snout. To discover what made these cars tick – in many cases not very much – I began reading weekly car magazines like *Autocar* and *Motor*. They reckoned the 18/22 was a potential world-beater, with its clever 'Hydragas' suspension, front-wheel drive, ballroom-sized interior and wedged, otherworldly styling. It certainly looked like the future to me.

These often rather dry magazines were the first things aimed at adults I'd read, but some of the writing in them was good, and I began imbibing this as much as the cars being written about. I'd come a long way from *Buster & Jet*.

None of this answered the question of where I was going to go next. Despite my mannered southern accent, which once caused Judith to ask why I pronounced 'grass' as 'grr-arse,' I'd experienced very little bullying, but there was still a feeling that I'd be eaten alive at the local comp. I still longed to 'go home,' but it was no longer clear where home was.

My parents by then were officially living apart. My mother was coping with life in the cottage, but looking after me was beyond her, and my dad was now permanently based at the large Hammersmith townhouse owned by his brother, where my Gran had a flat. He was also working madly long hours.

I liked the idea of living there because it would mean getting back to London, where I really felt at home, but was told this would be too much for my grandmother.

On one of his visits, Dad asked, with slightly staged casualness: 'What would you think about boarding school?'

I hated the idea. As a very small child when I'd heard about these places I developed an irrational fear that I might be sent to one of them. The idea that this long-held anxiety would be realised was not appealing.

'Would you have a look a boarding school, if we took you to visit it?'

I could hardly say no, and it turned out that my dad had a school in mind.

'It's called St Christopher's. It's in Hertfordshire, so you'll be closer to us. You don't have to wear a uniform, you call the teachers by their Christian names, and there are boys and girls. Some of the children sleep in huts. Oh yes, and it's vegetarian.'

My dad produced a small stapled brochure with grainy black and white pictures of these huts, an open-air swimming pool, a woodwork shop and some science labs. There was also a picture of the headmaster, a suited, handsome, grey-haired man in his fifties, looking squarely into the camera lens.

A few weeks later, he was showing us round the school,

and I was amused to see that he wore glasses, which had been removed for the photograph.

Largely built round a quad, the main building was Edwardian and rather attractive. The boarding houses that surrounded it were big handsome structures with arts and crafts touches. The huts, with their twin beds, had a pleasant timber and wood preservative tang. It was all very civilised. This was an institution working hard to function on a human scale, that was proud of its benign, progressive heritage, but it was an institution, and it filled me with dread. I hated the lack of privacy, hated the idea that I could never quite shut the door on school life, or have a breather from my peers. It wasn't that I felt superior to them, quite the reverse. I often felt as if I was running to catch up with the cut and thrust of school life, and the ability to escape from it and retreat into my own space provided respite that made dealing with it easier. Being forced to live constantly in a school was horrifying. I knew that this was not the place for me.

With my parents temporarily reunited and sitting in the waiting room, the headmaster called me into his office, with its parquet floor and polished wood-panelled walls.

'Would you like to come here?' he asked.

'No!' said a voice in my head, but he seemed like a nice man, and I did not want to be rude.

'I don't know,' I lied.

'Well, we'd very much like it if you did.'

When my dad finally drove me back to Lancashire I hadn't much to say. What had been sold to me as 'having a look at a boarding school' had turned into being sent to it.

'Try it for six weeks and see if you like it,' said my dad. 'If you don't like it after that, just tell us.'

I could hear him more easily because he'd been to a breaker's yard and bought the Triumph Herald a non-knackered differential; farting exhaust aside, it was now much quieter. I thought about what he'd said and tried to feel better.

I left Lancashire with barely a backward glance, unappreciative of how lucky I was to have been there. Now I see things rather differently.

Then I remained a sometimes verbose, socially immature child with a motoring monomania that for entirely inexplicable reasons other people sometimes found boring, and could not be dislodged from the belief that if the reasons for my all-encompassing fascination could just be explained to them, they would change their minds.

I'd arrived at Preston station 18 months before, academically and personally adrift, and left able to read and write and far more centred in my head. I had been more than tolerated, been cared for and given badly needed security. And I had been loved.

In a nebulous way I still wanted to rewind life to where it had been before the move to Bedfordshire, when my mother was well and I'd been comfortable in my surroundings. I vaguely felt that embracing the home I'd ended up in by default was somehow being disloyal to my parents, but I wasn't ready to appreciate that I had actually gained an extended family that would become precious and important.

Instead I blocked out the idea of boarding school and concentrated on the imminent six-week summer holiday, which mostly I would spend in London, with its familiar streets and endless cars, buses and taxis. What could be more exciting?

I sold the chickens, having been told that they couldn't come with me to boarding school, and said goodbye to my friends at the farm, including 'Number 7', a particularly laid back Frisian cow I'd been allowed to help milk.

'She's a good girl, and she never kicks,' explained the farmer.

At the end of term, Sir solemnly shook my hand then pointed a stubby finger at my nose.

'You've done very well because you've worked hard,' he said. 'Now you have to keep working hard.' His voice dropped to a menacing rumble. 'If you turn into a lazy, constipated pillock, you'll be hearing from me, and you don't want that!'

My last day at school did produce a feeling of loss, and something akin to a trembling lower lip moment, although the emotion of this was somewhat tempered when my harassed aunt discovered that I'd cut my own hair the evening before. Her irritation lasted most of the following day.

'Oh, really, Martin!' she'd said. 'You look lopsided. I am not pleased.' But when it was time for us to finally, properly say goodbye, she gave me a prolonged, tight hug.

# School Daze

The sound of half a dozen eleven- and twelve-year-old boys sharing a room during their first few nights at boarding school is one of muffled weeping, followed on subsequent nights by weeping and wanking.

When my dad had finally deposited me at the boarding house for the first time, with every item of clothing I possessed now containing name tags that he'd stitched into them, and residing in a large Victorian trunk with a domed lid that he'd bought from a junk shop, I felt as if a brick had ended up in the pit of my stomach.

I held on to him fiercely until the moment that he climbed into the Herald and drove away. I listened until the sound of its engine was finally subsumed in the swish of traffic, wept briefly, and then made for the downstairs room where I'd been billeted with five other recidivists.

I'd been given the top of an aged metal bunk bed. Its frame was a mass of chipped paint and scratches, the bed itself covered with a patterned blue and white counterpane that had the feel and look of limp carpet. It had a similar consistency to the sparse mats that were dotted about the room's hard polished wooden floor, which I soon discovered would trip you up or slide out from under your feet if you didn't treat them with respect. The walls had lightly chipped pea green plaster, and the room was lit by a single ceiling light, hidden in a hard plastic lampshade.

I had access to a couple of shelves for my clothes and a small Formica-topped locker for my private things, which included a top-loading battery cassette tape player which my dad had given me as a twelfth birthday present.

'It's a bargain because you have to hold down the fast forward button, but if you do that it works fine,' he'd said. I was enormously proud of this item and guarded it jealously.

A bearded, not quite rotund man in his thirties came into the room. He was a music teacher who was also a 'houseparent,' running the boarding house with his wife. He made soothing noises about being new to boarding school life, and since he'd been a pupil here himself, said he knew how it felt, and assured me that things would be fine. He seemed diffident and a little shy.

My roommates proved more voluble. There was a small pugnacious boy from Wales with a freckled face and a lot to say, a skinny boy with pipe cleaner limbs and nervous eyes, who shifted from one foot to the other and spoke with a piping voice, a languid boy who almost immediately revealed a talent for cartooning, a small olive-skinned character, and a self-contained boy with Dr. Martens boots and the profile of an Easter Island statue, who announced that he liked guns.

They fed us and put us to bed at 7.30, which seemed absurdly early, but then we were all getting up again at 6.30 the next morning for our daily communal morning walk. The school, founded in 1915, retained a very Edwardian enthusiasm for fresh air.

Out went the light, the Welsh boy whispered ruderies, we laughed, the door opened and an adult voice told us to be quiet. This process was repeated until the whispering stopped and the weeping began.

My recollection of boarding school life is one of sensory overload. Shoes clattering on hard floors because there weren't many carpets, vegetarian food with odd flavours and strange textures, noise and chatter between lessons, shoals of people moving from class to class, of having to dodge round the older pupils. Girls with grown-up shapes and boys, some with long hair and almost beards, who towered over you as they strode down the long submarine-like corridor that was the spine of the main school complex.

And to start with, being cold. This last recollection might be a little unfair, but the place had quite a lot of creaky infrastructure that was constantly patched and bodged by a collection of glum-faced maintenance men. This included feeble electric tube heaters in some of the classrooms, which packed up regularly, and since there was no law about how warm private school classrooms had to be, we'd sometimes shiver through lessons if they refused to be fixed quickly. Metal-framed chairs with canvas backs and bottoms would sometimes come apart at the seams, folding round their occupants. Those chairs would be welded back together over and over again, with unlovely crudity.

Assembly, or 'morning talk' was held in a big lap-wood hall, where we all trooped in and sat on lines of wooden benches, and had the potential excitement that some of those benches would object to this and collapse. The headmaster would be giving us a slightly abstruse homily about life, and often, in a vague sort of way, God, because the school's ethos was closely connected to Quakerism, when there would be a bang, a thud, and a bench leg would give way as six or seven children slid down and ended up in a tangled heap on the floor.

Generally dormitories weren't heated at night, and when things got really cold, you'd squeak when first wriggling between the frozen bedsheets. In some of the rooms, and in the prized two-person huts, waking up to ice on the inside of the windows wasn't uncommon during winter.

Then there was that communal pre-breakfast 'morning walk,' when the entire school trooped round in a circle, hands in pockets and breath frosting. In the winter of 1975, when I first arrived, we did this in the dark.

The short post-breakfast walk to school took us across an orchard of gnarled old apple trees and through the school car park, which every morning was filled with cars that as time passed became synonymous with their owners. These included a large and rather ugly early 1970s Opel Rekord estate with a brown vinyl interior. The outside was painted lime metallic green. Its owner wore a green corduroy jacket that didn't quite match the car. An immensely tall and thin man with a moustache-less beard, he looked like a cross between Abraham Lincoln and the character Shaggy from the *Scooby Doo* cartoons. He taught art.

An immaculate pale blue Rover 90 was owned by a thirty-something man with a gentle manner, a laughing cavalier beard and a solid, friendly golden labrador. He was one of the school's music teachers.

A tired air-cooled clatter would announce the arrival of the woodwork teacher's ancient, faded red Fiat 500 Giardiniera, a tiny estate car so old that it had what were accurately described as 'suicide' front doors that opened the 'wrong' way. Its owner was a large, slightly gnomic man with twinkling eyes and a slow, deliberate way of speaking.

The Fiat would often shudder to a halt next to a well-used Morris Oxford estate, a big car with white scabrous paint and a battle-scarred red leather interior. In it would be a distinctive middle-aged couple. The woman was tall and angular and taught Latin, her husband was quite a lot shorter, wore thick glasses, walked with clockwork precision, and radiated good humour. He was a published poet who taught English.

A neat young woman with glasses who taught biology drove an equally neat, newish Mini. A corpulent, suited piano tutor arrived in a suitably large Vauxhall Viscount, a car that, to me at least, shared its owner's double-chinned look.

One of the most intriguing cars was a younger and much better-looking Opel Rekord saloon, a handsome wine red vehicle that was driven by a scowling and very bald history teacher. He did not exude affability, but the car was interesting to a small nerdy boy because it had cloth seats, which made a change from the sticky vinyl still widely used in car interiors at the time, it was left-hand drive and had a bonnet which bulged strangely. Under this was a diesel engine, which in mid 1970s Britain was very unusual. Diesel engines were restricted to buses, vans and lorries. A diesel car was a real novelty. Other than Mercedes and Peugeot, almost nobody offered them, which is why the Opel was left-hand drive. Its grumpy-looking owner had been forced to buy it in mainland Europe.

The groundsman drove a dark blue Morris Minor van, which he sometimes started with a crank handle, because the battery was seven years old 'but still had a bit of life in it.' The headmaster owned a white Triumph TR6 sports car. Both it and the Minor were always immaculate.

Secondary education was going to be problematic for me wherever I went. Chronologically I was old enough for it, but had only been reading and writing effectively for about eighteen months. I was quite big for my age and sounded older than my years, but underneath was in many ways a lot younger, and had a tin ear for social signals (as in 'shut up about cars, will you?'). Many of my new schoolmates were intolerant of this and also socially and linguistically quite some way ahead of me, which was a mixed blessing. Within a month of being in their company I'd heard the word 'cunt' for the first time.

My memory had the flickering inconsistency of an electric light with a dodgy switch, my ability to daydream through lessons was finely honed, and I was calamitously disorganised, constantly losing pens, books and rulers as I shuffled between classes. Some children 'got' what the place was about and loved it. They found the freedom it gave them empowering and flourished as a result, but socially, emotionally and academically I simply couldn't hack it, and quickly fell behind. Left to my own devices my work collapsed, and I rediscovered the fatalistic, bottom-of-the-class mindset of expecting to fail.

The teaching was varied. Maths was taught by a spare desiccated man in his sixties with huge eyebrows and half-glasses whose arms had broken off, so he'd repaired them with string. He quickly rattled through problems that baffled me, but admit that you didn't understand, or that you'd lost your pen, and he would often reply 'good boy', and keep going.

His clothes were impregnated with chalk dust. He cycled to school, often with an aged plastic mac flapping behind him, beating his besweatered back, from which wisps of chalk dust eddied.

The corduroy-wearing art teacher seemed kind and a little distracted, and tended to vocalise what he was thinking without filtering it. Once he told the class of pre- and early teen philistines of which I was a part, 'sometimes I want to drill a hole in my head and see what's inside.' The dog-owning music teacher's lessons were fun; his quiet authority, enthusiasm and ability to unravel bits of music theory and make them interesting and understandable made the time go quickly and pleasurably.

Not so French lessons, run by a burly, bearded middle-aged Scot, who had a sharp wit, a capacity to roar and shout, and failed to preside over classes where complete anarchy reigned. For a little while I was shocked by the noise and the way this man was constantly undermined by those he was trying to teach. One boy climbed into a cupboard, where he could open and shut the drawer above it from inside, sliding it in and out until the French teacher eventually noticed and hauled him out again. Once when locked out of a class he charged the door and smashed the lock, thundering bull-like into the room. He looked terrifying but wasn't, and could be riled to the point of total apoplexy.

'You're all bloody white trash!' he bellowed after twenty minutes of needling and obstructiveness.

'Lazy little bastards living off handouts from daddy! Products of the British Empire, and what the bloody hell has Britain ever done in the world that's ever been bloody worthwhile?!'

'What about Rolls-Royce?' somebody crowed in a deliberately mannered voice. We drove this man mad, and enjoyed it.

Attached to the wall of the woodwork shed was a small coffin, in which a tube of plastic wood was fastened with a neat wooden stake. This proved that the woodwork teacher had a sense of humour, which mostly he managed to conceal when working. I found his lessons achingly boring, because he gave most of his time to the two or three boys in the class who had real carpentry talent. The rest of us often stood around with almost nothing to do. The chosen had access to the best tools, the best wood. Everyone else usually had scraps of his time and scraps of timber, but it was a mistake ever to call these offcuts 'scrap' to his face at the start of a lesson. If you did he would completely blank you for the rest of it.

After weeks of tedium I managed to knock together a small wooden box. Since I had failed to gain the woodwork teacher's attention or help, the result wasn't pretty. Seeing my effort, he picked it up and called the rest of the class to look at it.

'If I had made something like that, my woodwork teacher would have dropped it on the floor and smashed it,' he said, pretending to drop the box, catching and handing it back to me, then turning away.

Eventually he taught me to make an octagonal fruit bowl, but refused to do this until I agreed to say that I was making it for him, rather than as a present for my dad. I was proud of the end result and hoped for more input, but it never came, and at the end of the year I vowed never to darken his class again. Away from it he was interesting company and often sardonically funny, but for most of us he wasn't really a teacher, more a craftsman who taught when he felt like it.

Woodwork wasn't my least favourite subject. As a sedentary, uncoordinated sport hater, team games of all kinds were a trial, particularly football. The cold, the mud, the boredom and the exasperated, bellowed insults of the people who enjoyed this stuff and were good at it, as I thrashed at the ball or tackled people in my own team. They didn't want me, and I didn't want to be there, but we were stuck with each other.

Usually chosen last or second to last and put in defence, where I could do the least damage, my mind would wander off into car-themed byways, thinking about my dad's Bristol, still decaying outside the Bedfordshire cottage, or the news that Aunt Pat's Bedford van had recently died and she'd taken over Uncle Mick's Mini. Eventually the outside world would intrude. I would become aware of shouts and screams . . .

'Gurdon. Gurdon! GURDON!'

A thundering posse of ball-booting boys would be bearing down on me, and I was supposed to defend the goal along with one of the other un-chosen, like the very fat boy whose slight, frankly gnomic-looking dad taught physics, or the piping-voiced boy who shared my room, who was slightly more socially and academically inept than me and just as unsporting.

Could we save the day? No chance. We'd run in the ball's general direction, it would get past us, and if it found the back of the net there would be howls of rage, jeers and insults. 'You IDIOTS!'

A friend from that period claims that he once saw me run at the ball, jump over it and keep going. If I'd kicked it, God alone knew where it would have gone. Wherever it went the result would have been further humiliation. Once I accidentally found myself chasing it, moving like a demented Jacques

Tati puppet, when my hand connected with something solid and there was a cry of pain.

One of the footballing stars had run up behind me and I'd accidentally hit him in the eye with the knuckles of a wildly flapping hand. He spent the rest of the lesson seeking me out and telling me that he was going to 'fucking kill you afterwards.'

'That's right, you're going to fucking die, Gurdon,' hissed one of the other sporting heroes.

And yet the games master was very good. Short, spare, neat and middle-aged, he moved with the tidy grace of a ballroom dancer, came from Yorkshire, and like Sir had a short fuse, and was not above clouting boys who raised his ire, but his approach was realistic and inclusive. You didn't have to be good to get his professional attention, and get the best of it, but you did have to try. In my case in football that involved running around a lot and keeping out of the way.

The games master shared this egalitarian approach with the English teaching poet. There were plenty of people in his classes who found the subject as boring as I found football, but they were never marginalised or ridiculed. There was an effortlessness about this hunched, bespectacled academic that inspired confidence and gave him authority. I suspect that this high-minded man didn't find the scrawled, over-written and weirdly punctuated essays I produced particularly edifying, but if so he never made it obvious.

As 1975 expired and 1976 matured, Ford introduced the Fiesta, a compact little hatchback with the exciting novelty of front-wheel drive; filling it with a gallon of petrol would cost you 77p. In the pop charts The Brotherhood of Man's 'Save All Your Kisses for Me' and The Wurzels' 'Combine Harvester' were curling toes and selling well. A territorial spat with Iceland over fishing rights resulted in gunboats being deployed and became known as 'The Cod Wars,' Harold Wilson resigned as prime minister, and I remained an increasingly unhappy boarding school inmate.

The place was both frustratingly bureaucratic and genuinely democratic. There were elections for head boy and head girl, pupil committees for everything from a film club to a school magazine. There were concerts, speakers came to talk to us about politics and world affairs, and there were plenty of outside activities and trips. In April 1976, when George Murcell finally opened St George's Theatre with a production of *Twelfth Night*, the school organised a trip. The cast included Eric Porter and Jamie's mum, who acted under her stage name Elvi Hale and played Maria in a bustled dress, moving round the stage as if she was on wheels. So this was what my friend's parents did for a living when they weren't busking on 'consume and forget' TV.

This sort of thing was all very civilised, but for the lost and dysfunctional not necessarily civilising. Some of us took little part in these things, either through disinclination or passive resistance to being involved. To fill the gap we were quite capable of mutual brutalisation. In the circles I mixed in there was a lot of low level bullying that a number of the teachers either ignored, treated with sorrowful disgust or in all probability never even noticed.

So it was in our room, where the Welsh boy, who was socially a little more adept and better with his fists, grew to be the least bullied; a kingpin who was the most accomplished instigator of the verbal and physical unpleasantness that was a big part of our dynamic. He wasn't alone. When one of us was having a hard time the others tended to join in, because if this stuff was being done to someone else, it wasn't being done to you.

One boy had continence problems, and I remember the glee with which a pair of his soiled pants were hung from a light fitting for everyone to see.

We bullied each other and were in turn bullied or reviled by children further up the food chain, who were achieving in ways we simply couldn't get near. In that first year the only place that guaranteed escape was the toilet. At the weekend we were made to travel in pairs when visiting the shops in downtown Letchworth, and very occasionally even had to share baths. I struggled to get on with people, but could never get away from them (nor they from me). I knew very well that this was the wrong place for me, and after six weeks, when my dad came to visit, told him that I really hated it, and could I please go somewhere else? His answer came as an unwelcome surprise.

'Mart, it's too early to tell,' he said. 'Try it for another six weeks.'

This would become a weekly conversation until I gave up asking. Clearly I would not be leaving soon.

Looking back, the couple who ran that boarding house were sweet, gentle, cerebral and civilised people who simply couldn't get their heads round what made some of us tick. They wanted to see the best from us, but weren't necessarily great at dealing with our worst excesses. Some, although not all of us, were almost beyond their control. The house was always very clean, the food healthy, but beneath its organised exterior were pockets of low-level anarchy. *Lord of the Flies* lite with added tofu.

Probably a little depressed, I soon became prey to outbreaks of barely controlled fury that mixed with pure childish frustration and a hormonal bubbling that would eventually boil over into adolescence. I was easy to provoke and apparently amusing to watch when riled. Would I have dared to behave like this with my dad, Aunt Pat, Uncle Mick, or the sometimes terrifying Sir? Guess.

⊕ ⊕ ⊕

One cold Saturday morning in March I walked into a Letchworth newsagent and began flicking through a motoring magazine called *Car*.

On the cover was an impossibly modern-looking vehicle. It was large, low and had a hatchback body. The magazine said it was a Rover 3500, which seemed odd to me, as that car was a discreetly square-looking thing that sometimes had its spare wheel mounted on the boot lid. Finding the article about the new Rover I discovered that the car in the pictures was a prototype surreptitiously photographed as it was being tested. This piece of industrial espionage was exciting in itself. *Car* had the look and feel of a quality newspaper's colour supplement, which made it very different from the weekly motoring magazines I usually saw. It was filled with writers I hadn't encountered before. Mel Nichols, the magazine's Australian editor, wrote richly descriptive stories about driving exotic cars across Europe that read like little road trip novellas. People like George Bishop and Phil Llewellin could create funny, intelligent vignettes from something as banal as driving a Mitsubishi Colt. They had voices on the page that made you feel as if they were talking to you.

Then there was a rake-thin bearded man called LJK Setright, who looked like a character from a Jules Verne novel, and whose writing was as strange as his appearance. Their words were surrounded by amusing headlines and captions, and presented in classy layouts and typefaces. Skimming the pages I found a lot of what I was reading to be opinionated, some of it actively rude about cars like Volvos, which I'd always assumed to be nothing short of brilliant. This was both a little provoking and intriguing. *Car*'s 30p cover price was expensive, and since I only had 20p I'd have to wait until the following Saturday when

I would be issued with another 20p if I wanted to buy it. A week later that's what I did, and it was a decision that would change my life.

The school was located 39 miles from where my dad was living, closer still to the moribund cottage that contained my mother, but in a world without the internet, texts and mobile phones, where contact was limited to letters, a house phone or a very tired school pay phone in which two and ten pence coins jammed, it might as well have been 3,000, and I felt marooned and trapped.

As the world's first garden city Letchworth is actually a fascinating place architecturally and socially, a romantic utopian idea practically realised and a world away from much of today's vile and expedient housing developments. It had started off attracting visionaries and cranks whom George Orwell skewered with acidic precision in *The Road To Wigan Pier*, which contains a description of a bus ride through Letchworth in the late 1930s, enlivened by 'two dreadful looking old men' dressed in 'pistachio-coloured shirts and khaki shorts into which their huge bottoms were so tightly crammed that you could study every dimple.'

Although very brown at the edges by the mid '70s, some of Letchworth's aesthetic alternative vibe was still just about clinging on. The tree-lined avenues, open vistas and William Morris houses were intact, but despite the place being the home of Britain's first roundabout and the Ogle Design studios, from which sprang the Raleigh Chopper bicycle, Bond Bug, Reliant Scimitar, and yes, the Reliant Robin, to a twelve-year-old child who missed the noise and bustle of London, it seemed contrived, bland and stodgy, which was unfair.

It's also worth remembering that Letchworth was subject to

the passive, decaying scruffiness and lack of choice that afflicted much of the UK at the time. Fancy a coffee? There was a Wimpy Bar next to the station, or a tatty café that sold soggy sandwiches and lukewarm, weedy instant coffee with the flavour of condensed milk and condensation.

In common with most of Britain, Letchworth completely died on Sundays. Even the pubic loos were locked up. So *Car* magazine, which at the time was to its rivals rather as *Private Eye* was to *Punch*, rude and iconoclastic, became a monthly portal to the wider world, and brought a subversive, sophisticated journalistic eye to the subject that mattered more to me than almost anything else.

I even tuned in to LJK Setright's often wilfully abstruse writing. As mannered as his dress sense (canes, bowler hats and monocles) it stirred in allusions to literature, art and music, used words I'd never encountered, and married up these things to cars, how they looked, felt or were made. He could be an egotistical, grandstanding smartarse, and was a regular in *Private Eye*'s 'Pseuds Corner', but there was also a gleeful flourish to the writing. You could tell he loved working and kneading words and sentences into shape, and sharing what he knew. And he liked and owned Bristol cars, which meant a shared passion. Soon the monthly appearance of *Car* acted on my brain like a splash of colour in a grey world.

When the summer holidays finally rolled round, the prospect of six weeks of freedom was bliss.

I stayed at the tall three-storey Hammersmith townhouse where my 82-year-old grandmother had lived since 1947, and where my dad was now based.

Built for late Victorian Mr Pooter clones, by the time punk rock had begun to emerge in the public consciousness during

1976 with the likes of the Sex Pistols and The Damned cheerfully belching into the faces of The Brotherhood of Man, this
house was in an area that had become run down and like many
of its cohorts was divided into flats. Gran's home was actually
owned by my uncle, a commercial airline pilot who worked
abroad. Gran, who looked tall, fragile, stick-thin and severe,
pottered about in a cluttered basement flat, behind which was
a metal-framed conservatory, piled high with old newspapers,
magazines, including *Picture Post* and *Lilliput*, egg boxes, and
brittle old yoghurt cartons dating back to the 1960s. She was
a hoarder, and having experienced extreme poverty during
the Great Depression, parsimonious to a degree that I couldn't
even begin to understand. I'd never gone without the basics, so
had no conception of what lay behind her behaviour.

Up a flight of stairs at the front of the house was a self-
contained flat that was occupied by a succession of young professional types. If you kept climbing the dark narrow staircase
with walls that were still covered in ancient paper with intricate
raised patterns, hidden under layers of white paint, past Gran's
cluttered bedroom, you'd reach another landing, with doors
leading from it. One went to a large first-floor flat occupied by
a rotund, elderly Polish couple, another to a bedsit with a tiny
kitchen that contained an old lady who looked like a rakish
version of Gran. This was her sister Joan, who exuded a faded
chain-smoking glamour, was clearly on her uppers, and could
often be heard hammering away at a small manual typewriter,
knocking out a novel that none of us were allowed to see. Joan
had 'a past' that I wasn't allowed to know about. Relations
between the sisters were often tense.

As for the Polish couple, she had a Mrs Tiggywinkle quality,
he was short and round, wore suits whose buttons heaved at his
midriff, was very bald and far less avuncular than he looked.

Get this far and you were confronted by a modern dark
wood staircase that went to an attic bedroom which my dad

had commandeered. This room was a recent innovation, but perhaps because of a row with the builders had never been entirely finished, which meant one upright of the doorframe, the one where the lock would have gone, was missing. Through this gap it was possible to hear Joan battering her typewriter or the Polish tenants, who I discovered were quite bonkers, shouting at one another.

There were no spare bedrooms, so I shared the attic with my dad, semi-camping on an air mattress, but that didn't bother me. I'd known this house all my life, liked it, and it wasn't school.

Today, this part of Hammersmith is the preserve of the very wealthy, the streets crammed with big 4x4s, new-looking Minis and shiny people carriers, but in 1976 its streets were the preserve of ageing Mk2 Ford Cortinas.

These were often driven by young black men, who always seemed to be stopped by white policemen with grey walkie-talkies clipped to their black tunics, wearing domed helmets that made them look very old fashioned.

The streets were thronged with similarly ageing 1960s-era cars, looking tired and battle-scarred. Some had died and been abandoned, a perennial problem in those days. These vehicular ruins would sit and rot for months, until a local authority lorry with a big mechanical grab carted them away for scrap.

The nearest parade of shops comprised a pub, a chemist run by a Sikh gent in a suit, and a sparse hardware store outside which was what looked like a small petrol pump with a coin slot. This dispensed paraffin, and Gran frequently dispatched me with a plastic jerrycan to buy a gallon for the ancient pressed-tin heater she often used to warm her flat and heat a kettle. There was a convenience store, a newsagent and a large car spares shop amusingly called Universal Ball Bearings. Trading since 1907, it was filled with blokes who smoked, a high Edwardian counter and lots of dusty wooden shelving filled with bits of car. I recently went back and found that it had become a wine bar. Near where the paraffin pump had stood, I drank a coffee at one of the parade's pavement cafés.

This was far removed from the edgy, flyblown *Sweeney*-era London of 1976, where I spent happy days just wandering around. It was the year of a prolonged heatwave, when the grass turned crinkly brown, we saw television news footage of parched reservoirs and people queueing with kettles and saucepans at standpipes because the mains supply had been shut down, and politicians suggested sharing a bath 'with a friend,' to save water.

During those baking, still days I went into Central London and just drank in the environment or walked along the towpath by the River Thames. I was happy, because for the first time since I was nine years old I actually felt at home. As time passed my grandmother put me right on that. This was her house and I was a visitor, a guest who belonged somewhere else. It wasn't clear where that somewhere else might be, but there was a hint.

My dad was back in touch with his friend Ken, a cheerful-looking, goblin-faced man in his fifties with the sort of comb-over hairdo that that in the '70s didn't possess the comedic potential it would have now. He was otherwise vanity free.

They'd met in the late 1960s when both had Jowett cars. Although Ken's was the more exotic Jupiter sports model, it had the same mechanical bits as my dad's Javelin saloons and the same problems, so when he saw Ken fixing his Jupiter by the roadside and went to talk to him, a friendship built on mutual suffering was born.

Ken had since jettisoned his Jupiter, instead driving an aged but less troublesome Renault 4. He'd also moved onto a houseboat. About thirty foot long and immaculate, this was a cabin cruiser he'd converted, and was moored in a creek that flowed into the Thames in the outer London borough of Isleworth. We sat on the deck in the summer sunshine, drinking tea and reminiscing, and thought the same thing. This would be a very nice way to live.

We visited Ken on the motorcycle my dad had recently bought; this was a Honda Goldwing, a hefty, 1.0 litre touring bike with a beautifully engineered flat four water-cooled engine, shaft rather than chain drive, and a fake petrol tank which was actually a luggage storage area, as the fuel was contained in pods under the seat to lower this enormous bike's centre of gravity.

It was a very different proposition from the hirsute MZ, and Dad had sold the ever-reliable Triumph Herald estate to help pay for it.

The Goldwing sounded wonderful, had effortless performance and in winter wafted heat on to you from its giant engine. Thanks to an inadequate front tyre whose sidewalls were too weedy to support it on corners, the bike dumped Dad in the road not long after he'd bought it, but with decent tyres it handled far better than its size suggested.

We used it to holiday in northern Scotland, camping by lochs and whisking along undulating open rural roads, the bike making us part of the scenery in the way a car never could. Afterwards on the journey south I discovered that wearing moccasin shoes in a hailstorm was not a good idea, as their waterlogged leather more or less froze to my feet afterwards. Near Birmingham we were negotiating some roadworks and seemed very close to some plastic cones: too close for my iced right foot, which clouted one. The pain was intense but brief, the complete lack of sensation that followed it alarming, and the hobbling discomfort when we finally got to London and my feet thawed out was pretty excruciating too, but this had been a fantastic trip, whose discomforts and joys became part of our personal folklore.

Back at school my knowledge of cars and what the motor industry was up to increased along with my detachment from academic and personal advancement.

By 1977 I could tell you that Fiat instrument panels would have a black background with yellow numerals, because yellow on black was easier to read than anything else. If you asked me what 'Audi' meant I could have told you that it had started life as a Latin word for 'listen,' but despite months of lessons I could not play a scale on the guitar, I couldn't speak French and had no idea what logarithms were. I was, as one school report put it, 'completely at sea.'

Ford had launched the Mk4 Cortina, the Queen was celebrating her Silver Jubilee as head of state and a woman called Joyce McKinney chased a Mormon missionary from the US to Epsom, where he'd been hiding from her, and with a friend kidnapped him and tied him to a bed. The resultant trial became known as the 'sex in chains' case.

The 'Free George Davis' campaign, which postulated that Mr Davis had been wrongfully imprisoned for bank robbery, succeeded in getting him released, which then resulted in Mr Davis robbing a bank and getting banged up again.

At school, I was one of the pupils sent down for a stretch in a specially created bottom set, humiliatingly called '2Z.' It contained a lot of the people I'd shared the six room with when I'd first arrived. We were told with disingenuous firmness that this wasn't a sin bin class, and with hard work we could leave it again, but the teachers without portfolio or without enthusiasm who took our classes clearly didn't expect this. This was a sin bin and we all knew it. My sole academic achievement was managing to work my way to freedom. I was the only person to leave 2Z without being expelled.

Back in the academically rarefied atmosphere of '2Y', I discovered as my teens progressed that if I opened my mouth it seemed to have a magnetic attraction to my feet. I also committed the teenage sins of not listening to the right music, and not caring about clothes. I was clumsy, scruffy, grubby, verbally crass and increasingly angry, but could tell you that the original Ford Fiesta nearly had round headlamps because at pre-launch 'car clinics' Italian women said they liked them.

The school took a quorum of bright but troubled children, some with local authority funding, I suspect for philosophical and pragmatic reasons. Some could, and did, engage with what it offered. It broadened their horizons and gave them the freedom to succeed, but as time passed and the exam passing gymkhana sped up, those incapable of taking that freedom were left with very little. A fuzzy, inconsistent approach to duty of care meant that some of us more or less ran wild. 2Z might have finished but I was part of an underachieving rump, increasingly shovelled into containment classes to get us out of the way of exam streams. Teachers who took pleasure from seeing bright, responsive children developing, found themselves 'teaching' nebulous non-subjects like 'social studies' to an unhappy rabble. Confronted by the bored, the hormonal and in some cases the damaged, their wish to be somewhere else, and in some cases their contempt, was often easy to spot. We were aware of this; aware of the delight they took in our peers' successes, of what we could see were the first flowerings of adult friendships between them, and resented these things because we were excluded from them. And as we grew older, we made them pay for it, even when some of these people were as much refugees from life as we were.

The 1970s were fizzling to a close, with punk rock still blaring in the background, the subject of enjoyably apocalyptic 'civilisation is ending' newspaper stories. The economy lurched about like a drunk on an escalator and everyone seemed to be going on strike. We'd had the so called 'Winter of Discontent,' when places like Leicester Square were piled with rubbish, and my dad paid £500 for a dilapidated metal-hulled houseboat. It was going to need a lot of work. Ken was no longer 'up the creek' and had found moorings on the Thames itself, still in Isleworth, courtesy of the Third Osterley Sea Scouts, and my Pa moored his purchase in the next berth.

British Leyland, now led by a small South African business-man called Michael Edwardes, was in the middle of a fight to the death with the unions. Edwardes was shutting factories, including the Abingdon plant in Oxfordshire, which had been the home of MG sports cars since the 1920s. The aged but much loved MGB and Midget ('arthritic,' reckoned *Car*) would die with it. A battle over pay resulted in Edwardes making the cover of *Private Eye*, which carried a picture of him saying '3% or you die, Blitish worker johnny.' This ran with the headline 'NEW JAPANESE LOOK FOR BL', and for a variety of rea-sons probably wouldn't appear now.

I came to the conclusion that I wanted to be a motoring jour-nalist but would never get the chance, and that, as my French teacher had written in one school report, much to my dad's anguished fury, my being at this school 'wasted both my time and his.' I'd given up, concluding that I would have to leave before I really started learning, and since that wasn't on the cards I might as well arse about in class, since this seemed to make me more popular. So did giving a boy called Clive a black eye. Ironically, that punch was one of my few real successes at this herbivorous, peace-loving institution.

Clive was a weaselly character whose idea of fun was to tear up my mail and ask whether I'd been born because my parents 'had a Durex with a hole in it.'

'Say that again, and I'll hit you,' I said.

He knew I wasn't good at hitting people; I wasn't good at anything, so of course he did. I aimed at a spot about twelve inches behind the back of his head, swung from the hips and kept my fist straight. There was a satisfying 'splat' noise and my fist tingled as Clive flew backwards, making a loud bang as he connected with a wardrobe and slid to the floor.

'You hit me!' he said, rubbing his eye, which soon developed a large bruise as a memento of this encounter.

'Yes. I said I would.'

Later, one of the senior boys, a hefty bruiser, used the enormous lapels of my jacket to slide me up against a wall until my feet dangled in the air.

'You hit Clive, didn't you?' he hissed.

'Ye-es.'

Suddenly he smiled, dropped me and said 'well done!'

Later, one of the more exotic senior girls, a diaphanous swirling skirted beauty who normally wouldn't have given me the time of day, swished into my personal space and spoke.

'Did you hit Clive?'

I waited for a rebuke. For a brief moment she laid a delicate, very clean hand on my shoulder. By this stage my balls had more or less dropped, resulting in an entirely unreciprocated interest in the opposite sex. I wasn't used to this sort of close physical proximity to a girl, and so blushed.

The full lips parted into a warm, white-toothed smile.

'Good,' she said. 'He's a little bastard, isn't he?'

# Three Wheels Bad

Imagine that you are fourteen years old with your whole life ahead of you, and are convinced that you are about to die. Now imagine that you are in a very small car. It's made of plastic with the consistency of Tupperware, and because it only has one little wheel at the front, it rocks from side to side as it bounces and lurches over ruts and potholes. The car is travelling at 50mph, closing fast on a hairpin bend. If this were you, how would you feel? I felt sphincter-contractingly scared, which was a pity, because this was supposed to be fun. It was also my first introduction to the weird, very English world of the Reliant Robin three-wheeler, and it happened during my boarding school incarceration. For years the Robin and its forebears covered the UK's road network like chickenpox on a sick child, providing transport for the very poor, the very strange, or motorcyclists who'd never taken a four-wheeled car driving test. One of the peculiarities of post-Second World War British life was that an unstable three-wheeled car could be driven on a motorcycle licence.

The Reliant was one of those engineering ideas that was simply wrong, but the wrongness was not in its lack of a fourth wheel. Cars with one at the back and two at the front can be a lot of fun. Morgan started out building them, and latter-day trikes, like the Grinnall Scorpion, continue to entertain the sort of drivers who like wearing goggles and getting flies stuck between their teeth, but such cars tend to be for people with money. The Reliant was all about impoverishment.

You can thank Raleigh, the people who make bicycles, for the Robin's existence. In 1935 it launched a 750cc, twin-cylinder, four-seater car for £110 5s, whose design had one wheel at the front, an engine behind that, followed by the passengers, squashed into what space remained. Somebody at Raleigh had a sense of humour because this lethal sounding vehicle was called the 'Safety Seven'.

Its designer was one T.L. Williams, who made a van version of the Safety Seven under the Reliant name from the mid 1930s, and by 1953, when Raleigh had long since binned its car building ambitions, Reliant, operating from a factory in the gorgeous Staffordshire town of Tamworth, had filled the gap with its first three-wheeled car. This had an Austin 7 engine, the stylishness of a cardboard box and an equally ludicrous name. 'Regal'.

There was nothing regal about this device, but in broke, ration-hobbled Britain it was a wobbly step up from a bus queue or a motorcycle and sidecar. You can gauge its appeal by something my mother told me about her mid-1930s childhood, around the time Raleigh made the Safety Seven.

Her father had a motorcycle and sidecar, and when he, his wife and three daughters went out for a weekend picnic, my grandmother and one child would climb into the sidecar, another would clamber on to the motorcycle pillion, and they'd set off, leaving the third child to walk. About a mile into the journey one of the other children would be dropped off, the bike would go back for the child who was already walking, pick her up, catch up with the second walking child, who would switch with the third one. This relay would continue until they all reached the picnic spot, and the process would be reversed on the way home.

The Regal appeared in an era when many families still had no transport of their own, so it's easy to see why something that was relatively warm and dry, which seated four people and was cheap, would have a lot of appeal.

Adolf Hitler also shares some of the blame for creating a ready British market for three-wheelers. During the Second World War, the British army taught thousands of conscripted soldiers to ride motorcycles. Some were better at it than others. In peacetime, a generation of ex-soldiers, some of whom perhaps lacked natural ability when it came to riding motorcycles, could do so badly, and were thus a natural market for three-wheeled cars. Perhaps this partly explains why Reliant trikes often became synonymous with mad, bad and dangerous driving.

Many early owners were deeply cash-strapped, and the Regal was extraordinarily parsimonious to run, capable of going a long way on the period's rationed 'pool' petrol that had the combustibility of weasel urine. The Regal was cheap, nasty, and sold like hot cakes.

Its rivals included the Bond Minicar. Designed by aircraft engineer Laurie Bond, it had a clever, light alloy body which, to start with, did without doors, brake lights and rear suspension. Its one-cylinder, 197cc engine was mounted over the front wheel, which it drove with a chain. Later versions could be spun 180 degrees so the car could turn on its own length. Versions of this weird little vehicle survived into the mid 1960s, by which stage the original Mini had killed off most of the other budget three-wheeled economy putterers, such as the amusingly named 'Meadows Frisky' and the rash of German bubble cars like the Heinkel and Messerschmitt.

When Reliant ate Bond in 1969 it had the market to itself, and was, implausibly, the second biggest British-owed car maker, churning out 20,000 vehicles a year. By then it had inflicted 50,000 Regals on the world, now with light, flammable, and spectacularly ugly fibreglass bodies. However, it also built the rather elegant Scimitar GTE sports estate car, which had four wheels and a 3.0 V6 Ford engine, so it was quick, as Scimitar owner Princess Anne found as she began racking up speeding tickets in hers.

The Robin's arrival in 1973 was well timed. Britain was back in recession and gripped by the first fuel crisis. According to the AA, British motorists were having to pay over 38 pence for a gallon of petrol when the Robin appeared. Two years later it was over 72p a gallon.

Britain was looking scruffy, grumpy and broke. It was a bit like the 1950s again, this time without the optimism, but it was fertile ground for Reliant's über-stingy Robin trike that cost £10 per year to tax and was claimed to eke out 60mph 'on 2 Star petrol.' It looked modern but wasn't, essentially taking the hideous Regal's ageing substructure and very lightweight engine and clothing them in a little body that was actually rather neat.

This was thanks to an industrial design visionary, Tom Karen, the man behind the Scimitar, who'd designed everything from trucks to children's toys. In fact he thought up the original Raleigh Chopper bicycle, which, like the Reliant Robin, had stability issues, but became a seminal part of many 1970s childhoods.

A gentle, charming man, Karen grew up in the Czech industrial city of Brno, arriving in Britain as a refugee fleeing from the Nazis in 1942, so in a way, perhaps there was a connection between the styling of this ungainly, plastic British three-wheeled car and some of the Bohemian design sensibilities which blossomed in Czechoslovakia before 1939. Karen headed an industrial design consultancy called Ogle, based in Letchworth. This was also the place where I had that downhill encounter in the passenger seat of a Reliant Robin and afterwards felt, if not death's wings brush against me, then perhaps the backdraft caused by them flapping in my general direction.

The car belonged to a hedgehog-shaped man in his fifties, with NHS glasses, a pencil moustache and manic depression, which given that he worked as a mental hospital porter was cruelly ironic. He was a kind soul whose wife worked as a cleaner at my boarding school. She had a big heart, a lugubrious manner, quite a lot of medical ailments and a hulking, motorcycle-riding teenage son.

'He's got a visa for his crash helmet,' she said of the son. 'And bisexual boots.' She meant unisex boots, and I promise you I'm not making this up.

When this lady had most of her teeth removed, everyone hid from her blow by blow, or extraction by extraction-related conversation.

'They're too big for my mouth and they're stretching my face,' she explained. 'They're making my gums bleed too.' She pulled back her lips for emphasis. 'I shall have to get them shaved.'

One afternoon her husband's much polished, red Reliant Robin was sitting outside the school. He was sitting in it, and we got talking.

'You'd be amazed at how fast it goes,' he said, eyes glittering behind his thick glasses. 'Have you ever been in one?'

I said I hadn't, and when he asked if I'd like to be driven 'round the block,' it seemed rude to say no.

Which is how I found myself hurtling towards that down-hill hairpin bend. As we approached it he slammed the car into third gear, the engine howled and the car's tiny, incongruously sporting steering wheel was wrenched to the left, followed in short order by the rest of the car. I tensed and waited for it to roll over. Instead the Robin lurched a bit and its driver shot sideways so that he was looking at a wall of dashboard rather than the windscreen and his head almost ended up in my lap. Since we hadn't fallen over, he twitched the wheel to the straight ahead position and rose majestically, so that he could once again see where he was going.

Ten minutes later we were back at the boarding house, having survived a three-point turn into the path of a milk tanker. Later, his wife laughed merrily at the description of his sideways lurch.

'That's why he's never been able to pass a proper car test,' she said. 'We used to have a motorcycle and sidecar, and he had to lean to stop it falling over on the bends, but he never got out of the habit. It used to really surprise the car test examiners.'

It really shocked me, and I made a private promise to have nothing more to do with Reliant three-wheelers. It was a promise I would fail to keep.

# Wrong Turn

The corruption of the thing I loved, and the personal corruption that went with it, started one weekend in 1979 as a bored adolescent's prank, when I was fifteen.

I'd found that the policy of arseing about in class was paying off in terms of status amongst some of my peers, adult authority was patchy, so were the sanctions for misbehaving, and I'd started to make some of the people who used to bully me laugh. A few of them seemed to quite like me, so I kept going. I had no conception of where to stop, nor how unacceptable my behaviour was becoming, not that I wasn't told. Instead I thought it had a cartoonish quality. Often it didn't, and as I pushed further into the margins the school tacitly washed its hands of me.

For some reason it occurred to a friend and me that it would be fun to pretend we wanted to buy a car and be taken for a test drive in it. We'd say that we'd like to be chauffeured, which got round the problem of being too young to drive.

So on a Saturday afternoon we parked our bicycles in an alleyway, walked into a Renault showroom and asked about a model called the Renault 20, a large plush hatchback.

For some reason the salesman was entirely taken in by two scruffy teenage boys, so we climbed into the back of the car and took him for a ride. We found the encounter utterly hilarious, watching the man nod sagely when we told him that we liked the car, but that the chauffeur would need to drive it first, and did he have a business card we could take?

Over the ensuing weeks we repeated the trick at other

showrooms, amazed at the gullibility of the sales staff who willingly drove us about in their expensive new cars, but it wasn't long before the excitement began wearing thin. So I suggested conning an exotic car dealer, and getting a ride in something like a Porsche or a Ferrari. I found a dealer selling Porsches in London, and rang him up about trying a second-hand yellow 911 Carrera.

With access only to a clunky, unreliable coin-operated pay phone, which made a series of beeping noises before it put a call through, assuming the coins that made it work didn't jam first, I needed a method of circumnavigating the thing and still making the call.

It was possible to ring the operator, claim that coins had jammed and ask to be connected for the amount that you'd 'lost.' This was theft, but untraceable, and got round the sound of pips at the beginning and end of the call and coins being spoon fed into the phone, as the operator connected you wordlessly and seamlessly. You just had to make sure the call didn't overrun.

This time I was in the company of a tall, excessively neat boy who'd adopted the persona of a demented old fogey and enjoyed listening to Wagner and, rather unexpectedly, Liberace. He also wore a brace and would enliven some lessons by laughing like a donkey and deliberately spitting it out. I arranged to try the car, which meant getting to London on the train. This presented another challenge. We didn't have enough money for the fare. So we bought tickets for a station a couple of stops up the line.

'I'll wear my Pierre Cardin suit,' said the Boy with the Brace, who pronounced 'Cardin' as 'Car-din.' 'That will impress them.' We got on the train and made our way to a first-class compartment, the better to get into the mood of being Porsche owners.

We shared it with a black couple. When the inspector came in, they were given a very hard time for not having the right tickets. We said, 'Oh dear, this might apply to us as well,' and that we 'might, just possibly, have overshot our stop,' which would mean going to King's Cross and taking a train back.

We were clearly a pair of well-spoken idiots, and the inspector was positively charming. He said this wouldn't be a problem.

At King's Cross we were left to wait for the return train. When the nice ticket inspector departed, we went to the end of the platform, using a wooden walkway illegally crossed the tracks to an adjacent empty platform, and walked through the unmanned barrier into the station concourse and out onto the street, where we were able to catch a bus pretty much to the showroom.

The salesman greeted us with unctuous civility, and apparently didn't smell a rat in two very young 'men' asking to be driven in a sports car rather than drive it themselves. The Porsche howled pleasurably up and down a stretch of dual carriageway, we said 'we'd think about it,' then caught the bus back to the station, dodged our way onto the platform and caught a train where a different, but equally credulous inspector believed our station overshooting story and let us off – or perhaps he didn't believe us but couldn't be bothered to make an issue of it.

Later on we sniggered as we dissected the day's events: what the salesman and rail staff had all said to us; how we'd had a very amusing day in London; and what we might do next to top this experience.

But what?

Every week I went to London for 'maths coaching,' overseen by a psychologist who'd helped my mother through a period of depression in the 1960s, and had become a family friend. By then in her eighties and consulting from a plush flat on New Cavendish Street, near the BBC, she had a charisma that came from great, un-showy intelligence and an interest in people.

We drank tea, ate expensive shortbread biscuits, and ground through mathematical problems whilst my mind wandered to the sounds of the traffic outside, listening to the engines of the cars, buses and taxis, trying to identify them by ear and every so often sneaking a look through the window to see if I was right in matching vehicles to sounds.

I loved being in London, away from the abrasions of boarding school, listening to this woman's soft, thoughtful voice, working through the interlocking mathematical questions as she pointed at a lined exercise book with tiny, neat hands with skin like parchment, laced with blue/green veins. She seemed impossibly old and wise, operating on a higher level than me, and it felt good to have her attention.

Once the coaching was over I didn't hurry back to school, and instead would wander round the busy streets, find a café, sit and slowly drink a cup of stewed tea and revel in being able to escape.

Every week I was given cash to buy the rail ticket to London and fiddled the amount slightly so there was a little money left over. Sometimes this allowed me to take one of the ageing red or silver District Line trains to Richmond and walk along the river towpath to where my dad's houseboat was moored. As this was a weekday and he was at work, I'd sit on the deck, watch the river traffic, ducks and geese and feel completely immersed in an environment that I loved. Eventually I'd start the return journey, stopping at a chippie for a greasy, carnivorously pleasing sausage and a bag of chips, which I'd eat as I walked along the towpath back to the station.

I'd finally roll up at the school at about 8p.m., which conveniently missed prep, and since nobody asked where I'd been in the hours since the maths coaching had finished, these excursions became fixtures of my week.

But the corruption was never far away, and after maths coaching on a balmy summer's day I went for another test drive in London, turning up at a new car dealer near Regent's Park and asking to try a brand new Rover 2600.

The Rover was sleekly modern and painted a matt yellow that now wouldn't look out of place on a council dustcart, but in the

1970s was all the rage in furnishings and clothes. The blazer-wearing salesman with the military bearing never questioned whether I was anything other than a genuine buyer. The car felt, and even smelled expensive and new, and it was an automatic, which is why, when we were passing Regent's Park Zoo and he asked if I'd like to drive it, I said yes.

I still couldn't handle a manual car because I'd never mastered a clutch, but I'd watched other people driving and was confident that I could control a car that changed its own gears. And so it proved. The Rover was very easy to drive, and the Regent's Park ring road was quite lightly trafficked. As we trickled past the newly built Regent's Park Mosque with its copper dome glittering in the sunlight, I shut out any thoughts of what might happen if this went wrong, if we had an accident, and someone was hurt or killed. Instead, I was beside myself with excitement. At school I felt useless but I knew about cars, and suddenly I could drive one in the middle of London. How many of my peers could do that?

A Humber Imperial limousine swung out behind us. It looked like the car then taking former Liberal Party leader Jeremy Thorpe to court. Thorpe had been charged with attempting to murder Norman Scott, a man claimed to be his lover. Scott's dog, Rinka, had been shot in mysterious circumstances. This was 1979, and one of the year's biggest stories, and the cause of much tasteless British humour ('vote Liberal or we'll shoot your dog' was a popular joke at the time), so when I said it looked as if Thorpe was following us, the salesman laughed dutifully.

I did not come to grief on that drive, took the salesman's business card, said I was interested in the car, but wanted to try a Ford Granada. The salesman said he quite understood, and I melted into the London crowds, trembling with adrenaline, and keen to repeat this illicit experience.

So I did, and when this happened a round-faced, sullen-looking boy with a Welsh name came along for the ride. Having an audience was part of this teenage ego trip. It was a couple of weeks later and we'd booked a test drive in a Ford Granada, having hidden our bicycles and walked into another showroom with a squeaky floor. Soon I was again behind the wheel of a powerful, expensive car.

The drive lasted barely ten minutes. Terrified but vibrating with excitement, we sped along a straight stretch of road, made a slightly awkward turn at a roundabout, sped back, and managed not to clout any parked vehicles as I nosed the big Ford through busy, built-up side streets and back to the showroom.

'We've got to try a Rover 2600, but we'll think about it and let you know.'

It should have stopped there, and of course should never have got so far in the first place, but even then, I think I knew that it wouldn't. What next? What if we could buy a car, hide it somewhere and drive it around? Soon afterwards I saw a red Triumph Herald sitting in a front garden with a 'For Sale' sign on it. The owner wanted £30 for the car because it had a rusty underside and was not, he felt, worth fixing.

Triumph Heralds were so easy to drive that they had been favourites of 1960s driving instructors. So the Boy with the Brace and I took this one for a test drive, and for the very first time I mastered a clutch. The vendor lived close to the school, it was a total fluke that nobody saw us, and we left intoxicated by the idea of having access to this experience whenever we wanted.

We wanted it quickly, and knew that finding odd jobs to raise the funds was out of the question. This wouldn't be allowed and anyway, we were unemployable. At this point the final corruption happened. What if we stole something to pay for it?

I can't remember who broached the idea, but I wasn't led, wasn't coerced. When it was put into words the idea was already in my mind. The school had a music block, with a windowless room filled with musical instruments that was never locked. We'd take one and sell it in London, or rather I would commit the theft and my 'friend' would stand guard outside. He'd be a virtual thief, which, given that I heard he'd later joined the police, at least provided him with a first-hand insight into the criminal mind, but I'd be the real thing. So one afternoon I became a criminal and stole a flute, and a few days later took it to London and sold it in a music shop near Tottenham Court Road, probably during one of the maths coaching trips.

Once I decamped to London for a whole day. There was the initial terror of what my father would say when he found out, but he didn't because nobody brought me to book, perhaps because they hadn't noticed, or in some cases were glad to be free of my awkward, disruptive presence. This was an extension of the lack of enquiry that allowed me to vanish for hours after the maths coaching, and perhaps a mindset that expected someone of my age to take responsibility for his actions. Most of my contemporaries did. Many were blossoming and finding their feet because of the way the school did things. They loved and made good use of the freedom it gave them, and on a corporate level it loved some of them in return.

There was also a philosophical element; trusting pupils was part of what the place did, was good for their self-esteem and would encourage them to do the right thing, and if they didn't, sticking with them for long enough would see things right in the end. I'm sure this was sincere, but it didn't work for everyone, and for those who needed very definite external discipline and boundaries, it sometimes amounted to neglect.

So the school provided a roof over my head, fed me and offered an education if I chose to take it, but did nothing consistently if I didn't.

There were events that were just funny. One of them involved an illicit pack of Wall's sausages.

In common with a lot of 1970s institutional catering, the school's food was varied, though it was exclusively vegetarian, another aspect of its humane approach to the world that many of its carnivorous inmates found a mixed blessing. New arrivals in particular often hated this very healthy diet, and at weekends or holidays would devour almost anything with any meat content, as long as it wasn't actually twitching.

Today, a lot of vegetarian cuisine is great, because people know how to cook it, but in the 1970s the average chef hadn't the foggiest notion, and whilst the stuff we were given was nutritious, it was often bland, damp, bubbling or rubbery.

There was a foul red stew called 'protoveg' with the texture of mud and the odour of dog mess, which was slopped onto our plates from rectangular metal vats by a charming Chinese chef. He didn't speak much English, but to cheer us up would sometimes detach his front false teeth, shove them forward so he looked like a demented rabbit, and do a little jig uttering the words 'Mr Mo! Disco dance!' Then one day the teeth shot out of his mouth and landed in the protoveg, so it, rather than Mr Mo, was smiling at us.

There was shortbread that was so solid it could have insulated walls, on which a dollop of cold green apple purée was deposited. Smashed into pieces with a knife and spoon, this actually tasted quite nice, but on more than one occasion plates were shattered in the attempts at breaking it up.

There was still that awful habit of trying to make grey soya resemble meat products like sausages, which it failed to do. Our diets contained a lot of salad, nuts, dried fruit, and potatoes, often not entirely peeled, because they were reckoned to have the greatest goodness just under the skin. So the nastiest processed meat products were prized by some of us. Which is how a friend and I found ourselves in the kitchen of the boarding house where the youngest pupils were incarcerated, cooking four Wall's sausages, and peering over our shoulders through the kitchen window in case we were discovered. The sausages were nearly done when we saw a rapidly approaching teacher. Thinking quickly, but only thinking up to a point, we yanked the bangers from the spitting, smoking pan, shook some of the grease from their sizzling exteriors and stuffed them into our trouser pockets. A door banged open and the teacher bustled into the room.

'What are you doing?' She sounded suspicious, and began sniffing the air like a hunting dog, inhaling sausages and a light mist of fat particles.

'We were going to make some fried bread.'

'Can I smell meat?' The teacher gave us both a penetrating look.

We shook our heads and said nothing. We had other things on our minds. The sausages were now cooking us through our trouser pockets, and this was beginning to hurt like hell. My eyes had started to water, and my friend wore a look of extreme concentration. If this stand-off continued, how long would we be able to bear the pain, and would the sausage smell eventually be joined by the stench of fried schoolboys?

'Well, then,' she said at last, in a tone of studied disbelief. 'I won't keep you,'

Afterwards we hauled the still red-hot sausages from our pockets, slapped them gratefully onto a work surface and rubbed our lightly cooked flanks, which for weeks afterwards were to bear rouged, sausage-shaped welts, mirrored by the grease imprints we never quite managed to wash out from our trouser pockets.

The sausages themselves were now coated with a kind of bum fluff of nylon and trouser fuzz, but we were able to scrape most of this away. Then we dropped our prizes back into the pan. We weren't going to waste them.

On the train back from fencing the flute, the money from the theft in my pocket, next to the now fading sausage scars, I knew this time I would eventually be caught, and the consequences would be serious, but on one level I wanted it to happen, because I wanted all this to stop, and having the capacity not to take responsibility, wanted others to do this for me. I was also driven by a morality-free selfishness, which decades later I can't begin to justify. To rationalise and try to explain something like this without it reading as if the subtext is explaining it away is beyond me, but to the middle-aged adult I am now it smacks of a grotesque form of attention seeking, and on that level it was to be completely successful.

Later I walked from the station to the house with the red Triumph Herald, paid the owner and drove the car to a side street. It would take another three weeks for the school to find out what I'd done.

Five of us knew about the car. The Boy with the Brace, the Boy with the Welsh Name, the sausage Boy Who Wanted to be a Barrister (and sensibly wanted nothing to do with it), and the Boy with the Spiky Hair, a languid, socially sophisticated and attractively dangerous character. He smoked, had girlfriends and a cruel streak, but in the teenage social dynamic of which I was finally, slowly becoming a part, without even beginning to understand it, he was near the top of the hierarchy, and to be liked by him conferred status. Did he like me? Up to a point perhaps. This was a situational friendship, but I could make him laugh, and of course, I had a car.

'We could go to London in that,' he said.

This was true, but only with enough petrol in the tank; we had no money, and it was nearly empty.

'I could siphon some from the school minibus,' I said.

The Boy with the Spiky Hair smiled. 'You could at that.'

After 'lights out,' at about eleven at night, in pyjamas under my outdoor clothes, I made my way to the hedge where I'd stashed a plastic jerrycan that had once held kitchen fat and the length of tubing I'd appropriated from the chemistry lab, and made my way to the school's tatty Ford Transit minibus.

The sky was clear and the moon bright, so seeing what I was doing was easy. I stuffed the hose into the filler neck, put my lips to it and sucked up the fuel, gagging as acrid Four Star burned the inside of my mouth. I then dropped the pipe into the can and watched the liquid, which in the dark looked like urine, as it rumbled out.

Then I heard footsteps, and realised that they were getting closer. Running away would attract attention, so I wriggled under the minibus, pressing myself against the dusty tarmac. I recognised the voices as the headmaster and a colleague. They were talking and laughing. They stopped when they reached the minibus.

Had they seen the can? Breathing heavily I kept still and tried not to shrink back. Then I became aware that the ground was wet. The petrol was overflowing from the can and spreading under the minibus, soaking my clothes and staining my hands with tar. Everything stank of fuel. Would they smell it and investigate?

I waited. More laughter, then the sound of receding footsteps. I stayed under the minibus for as long as I could bear, emerged, yanked out the tube, re-attached the filler cap, hid the can in a hedge and crept back to bed.

My hands were black, my clothes discoloured and I reeked of petrol, but I didn't dare wash. That too would attract attention, so I got up very early and gratefully showered. Since I did my own laundry I was able to hand wash my clothes, and the following night I retrieved the can and filled up the car. There still wasn't enough fuel, so back I went the following night, and this time wasn't disturbed. It was late, the buildings were bathed in light and I could hear noise. Drawing nearer I realised it was the fire alarm. I was wearing pyjamas under my outdoor clothes, which I pulled off and stuffed into a hedge with the jerrycan and tube, then I ran back the way I'd come and joined the pupils who were now spilling out of the dormitories. Like me, many had outdoor shoes, so I didn't stand out. A teacher ticked my name on a register. When it was announced that this had been a false alarm, we trooped back to bed.

At midnight I was again on the school field, pulling dew-damp clothing over my pyjamas. I crept through the golf course that separated the school from where the car was parked, emptied the can into its tank, dumped this in the boot and slipped back into the dark.

The Boy with the Spiky Hair and I had plans to burn it on a trip to London. We had a games lesson followed by something that was euphemistically described as a study period, which effectively meant the afternoon was ours. Rather than spend an excruciating hour on the football field we'd elected to 'go for a run,' and trotted off holding in our stomachs the better to hide the clothes we'd concealed under our violent green gym sweaters. Once out of sight we changed and made for the car.

By now the theft of the flute had been discovered. It belonged to another pupil, a girl a couple of years younger than we were, who, unlike some of her contemporaries, still looked like the child she was. The flute was a thing, but its owner was a person, and I now knew what she looked and sounded like, and knew also that what I'd done had been done to someone.

Her loss was announced in assembly, as I knew that it would be, and for a while I did feel a sense of guilt because this was no longer abstract, but quickly discovered a capacity for self-deception and compartmentalising feelings for my own convenience. This meant that I actually began feeling sorry for her, as if what had happened had nothing to do with me. Sorry. This was an obscenity and a further corruption, intended to shut out personal responsibility. Soon I did this by not thinking about her.

I didn't think about her as the Boy with the Spiky Hair and I climbed into the Triumph Herald. It had a wooden dashboard with knobs and toggle switches scattered about on it, and a speedometer the size of an old fashioned bedside alarm clock. To start it I pulled out one of the knobs, the choke, pressed the accelerator and turned the small chrome ignition key, the starter motor churned and its engine puttered into life.

As the Herald vibrated gently the vinyl seats felt cold, the big plastic steering wheel slim and hard. I slipped the car into gear, released the handbrake, let out the clutch, and we were on our way.

In 1979 there was no congestion charge, no police national computer, no cameras to record car registrations and check whether they're road legal and insured. The Herald looked respectable and unremarkable, and up to a point, so did we. Unless we did something stupid, nobody would notice us.

To write about the journey to London and ones that followed is difficult, because they were exciting, of course they were, and the negatives, the danger, irresponsibility and gulling of authority, the sheer wrongness of what we were doing, was part of that excitement. These things were coupled with a sense of freedom and escape.

We went to visit the Boy with the Spiky Hair's mother, who lived in a plush London town house, driving along Kensington High Street and past expensive West Brompton villas to where she lived. We overshot the road, U-turned in front of a taxi, parked and went in for a coffee.

She didn't see the car, and I can't remember what lies we told about how we'd got there, or what we were doing, but she didn't seem that interested. We were back in time for prep, unscathed and feeling very pleased with ourselves.

I rarely drove that car alone, taking it out most frequently with the Boy with the Brace. At one point we were followed by a police car, and almost wet ourselves with terror. After a couple of weeks I knew this addiction had to stop, and the way to do this would be to scrap the car, but I would need the registration documents, which had been sent to my mother's house. By this stage she'd withdrawn almost completely, no longer wrote, answered or opened letters. Her life had shrunk around her. It was a reductive shroud of waking, eating, shopping and sleeping. She'd also become prey to paranoia that her close family members were imposters. That this extended to her sisters and me was the subject of much grief. The fact that I didn't see her for months on end and had changed a lot physically only stoked this anxiety, and made visiting her painful and unsettling, so increasingly I didn't. If I was to dispose of the car I'd have to, but the bloody thing was so intoxicating, and I kept driving it.

'A red Triumph Herald,' said the man running the senior boarding house where I now had a single room.

'I want the keys, and I want the rotor arm.'

One of the kitchen staff had seen me in the car and asked whether this was right. It was 10.30 on a weekday night when I'd been summoned to the houseparent's flat. Afterward, I put on my outside clothes, went out into the night, unaccompanied, got the rotor arm, handed it over, and then walked to the headmaster's house and banged on the door. He was wearing a dressing gown when he opened it. He looked shocked.

'What on earth are you doing?'

I told him about the car, and how it had been paid for.

Perhaps this voluntary confession was why I wasn't expelled, why the police were never called, the rest of the staff not told exactly how I'd come to acquire the car. A year later the information started leaking out, and I have no right to complain about the cold fury it provoked in a couple of the teachers. I suspect some calculations about the damage chucking me out might do to the school, along with a genuine wish to give me another chance, and not blight what future I might have, were also involved in that decision. However humane and well intentioned, it was a mistake. I was bad for that school and it was bad for me, and we should have parted company.

There were consequences. That I was capable of something like this caused my father immense pain, and it made relations between us very rocky for a while. He paid for another flute. The school year ended, a tense summer holiday ensued.

My cruelty, selfishness and recklessness, and their consequences (and potential consequences), were forcefully pointed out to me, but I'm not sure I had the empathy to grasp what was being said. I've heard kids on TV, who've gone off the rails, using stock phrases of apology, the official language of contrition, and wondered if they really meant those words, even if they thought they did, or whether they were parroting formulas for making unpleasantness go away. In my case both those things applied. It's no justification, but I'm sorry now.

# Last Stand

When I returned to the school in the autumn, it was utterly traumatised. The headmaster was dead. Riding a bicycle while holidaying in Malta, he'd been hit by a truck and killed. He was in his late fifties and his father had been the school's first head, so his life and its were entirely bound together.

As the place grieved I slithered towards academic catastrophe, and as before was largely left unchecked, so as the year progressed I gradually went back to my truanting, lesson-skipping ways.

Some of us had taken to home brewing, using illicit glass demijohn bottles filled with water and yeast. By now I had been deposited in one of about thirty first-storey single rooms called 'the cells,' because there was something slightly prison-like about the way all their doors radiated off a long corridor. Inside each was a bed, a double wardrobe, a chair and a desk by the window, and underneath that was a continuous radiator pipe that ran through all the cells. This was an ideal heat source to ferment illicit home brew, and even the Boy Who Wanted to be a Barrister had decided that it would be fun to make some of this stuff, and bought a brewing kit.

At one end of the cells was a flat occupied by a member of staff. It used to be the home of the grumpy history teacher, who allegedly quite liked a drink himself. Some years before I'd arrived there he'd woken up after a heavy night to find that his door had been bricked up by his charges. Apparently he was not amused.

Now the flat housed a thirty-something science teacher. In

profile, this short, stocky, bearded man had the sort of face you'd see on an ancient Greek vase. We called him 'Chop Chop' because he was a karate enthusiast, who when walking down corridors would suddenly kick the walls with little dancing movements while chopping them with the sides of his hands. He had a slight blonde girlfriend whom we christened 'the Blancmange,' for reasons I never discovered.

'Where's Chop Chop?' someone would ask.

'Oh, poking the Blancmange,' was the usual reply. We were pretty horrible.

Speaking of horrible, a few days after the putative barrister started home brewing, the unlovely Clive, who'd concocted his own hooch a few days before, drank it. Then he drank the sediment and was violently sick in the corridor, right outside the barrister's door. Knowing that the demijohn would be in full view under the desk, and that he was out, I stepped over the prone, gagging Clive and the luminous orange contents of his stomach, hid the evidence in the wardrobe and emerged just before Chop Chop came steaming into view, shouting,

'What the bloody hell's going on here?'

He was closely followed by the barrister, who, convinced that he was about to be in serious shit, scuttled past Chop Chop, vaulted into his room and stood in front of where he thought the demijohn still was.

The door smashed open, and there stood Chop Chop, looking like an angry bull. He tried to see past the Boy Who Wanted to be a Barrister, who stayed where he was until Chop Chop shoved him out of the way and peered under the empty desk. The barrister's look of incredulity was priceless.

Chop Chop gave him an unfriendly scowl, then said, with more accuracy than he knew, 'This room smells like a bloody brewery!' Wrenching open a cupboard door he added, 'And I'm going to take it apart brick by bloody brick until I find out why.'

He'd opened the wrong cupboard door, and was about to

open the right one when Clive moaned 'I feel ill!' and was violently sick again.

'Oh Christ!' said Chop Chop and went to mop him up.

When he'd gone we wrapped the demijohn in an old jacket. The demijohn had a non-return valve that was now making 'bloop, bloop, bloop' noises. There was a fire door at one end of the corridor, which I opened, and carried this incriminating object into a classroom, which was being used for a German evening class. I smiled weakly at the surprised linguists, and made a hasty exit. It was dark, so I walked to the boarding house containing the very youngest pupils, which was run by a small, glamorous woman called Sheila, who'd been a matron when I'd first arrived and had become an unlikely ally. For some reason she saw me as a child who still needed looking after rather than a young adult who'd gone bad and was beyond control, which was the reputation I'd gained elsewhere.

'I will only do this once,' said Sheila, shoving the demijohn under a bed in the appropriately named sick room. When its contents were ready the barrister and I decided we needed bottles to contain the result. We liberated some from the kitchens that had contained Stergene detergent, did our best to wash them, and then poured in the dull brown liquid. When we poured it out again the beer had a prodigious head, which bubbled and frothed down the side of the glasses. We drank it anyway, giving up when the Stergene-induced stomach cramps kicked in, but at least we didn't drink the sediment.

Sheila was both very maternal and a femme fatale. She had been married three times, but got on well with her exes, who, along with their wives, girlfriends and new families would descend on her every Christmas. She certainly had a habit of collecting life's waifs and strays, including me.

Her flat became a bolt hole, a place I'd go to cool down after I'd fucked up in some way, or to enjoy the novelty of being in the company of an adult who seemed pleased to see me. There was fondness I'm sure, but also great kindness and patience.

I'd developed a lippy bravado that hid the fact that I was bloody scared. Life seemed to be out of control and I was prey to nebulous anxieties and terrors that kept me awake late into the night, reading or re-reading *Car* magazine with a torch, or clamping a small transistor radio to my ear and filling my head with the late night chatter of the World Service. When I couldn't sleep at all I would go for nocturnal walks, sometimes turning up at Sheila's doorstop very late at night. She would make coffee, talk to me and send me back.

She had a boyfriend, or more specifically a man friend. He worked in the London jewellery business, possessed a grey-haired, middle-aged sleekness, and drove a new Rover 3500S, whose gold coloured alloy wheels meant that it was one of the first 1,000 made. This was something I felt he would be fascinated to know.

'He's quite jealous,' said Sheila.

On one of my night-time visits he appeared at the door not long after I'd arrived. The atmosphere seemed strange.

'I'd like a drink,' he said, 'and I'm sure Martin would like one too. How about a gin and tonic, Martin?'

Well, of course I said yes.

What Sheila thought about this was left unspoken, because the Jeweller rapidly mixed the drinks, handing me a large tumbler filled with clear, bubble-free liquid. It tasted powerful and strangely flat. After five minutes Sheila said, brightly but firmly, 'I think it's time to say goodbye.'

'Are you going out?' I asked.

'No,' she said. 'You are.'

I gulped down my strange G&T, stood up, and had to make several refusals before the Jeweller could be persuaded that I did not, after all, want another. About five minutes later the drunkenness hit me. It felt as if I'd walked into a wall. I'd been given neat gin, and weaved back to my bed, wondering why.

'Are you all right?' asked Sheila, when I saw her next.

Apparently the Jeweller regarded me as a love rival, and was attempting to extract a drunken admission of hanky-panky between me and his 45-year-old girlfriend, whose job was looking after other people's children, and would no more want to lay an inappropriate finger on me than stick pins in her eyes.

Although Sheila told me that the Jeweller was capable of feeling threatened by almost anything with trousers and a pulse, this revelation was alarming yet strangely gratifying. What she said next pleased me too.

'Mind you, he didn't know his car was special until you told him. He's delighted.'

Yes, I put the Mini on the cricket square, but I had a little help.

The car was an ancient, early 1960s Traveller estate, owned by yet another member of kitchen staff. It had a fibreglass front because the original panels had rotted away, and the woodwork that decorated its sides was becoming frilly too. It was probably no more than an MOT away from the breakers, but of course now would be a prime candidate for restoration, as in mint condition such a car would be worth five figures.

A lot of cars that were similarly old, such as the knackered Ford Anglia the woodwork teacher had bought to replace his knackered Fiat 500, used small single-edged keys, which were often duplicated. In 1980, if you liberated a few sets from wrecks in a breaker's yard the chances were that they'd fit plenty of others that were still going. The school car park was filled with cars like this.

I had friends now. Some, like the Boy with the Spiky Hair,

were considered a bad lot by some of those in authority, which was part of their appeal to everyone else. I was very much an acolyte, on the periphery of a teenage social mêlée, but I was no longer completely excluded from it. Most of those friendships haven't endured, but one that did was perhaps the most unlikely. The friend in question was called David. A compact, tough, teenage alpha male, he made his presence felt early in his school career by breaking someone's nose. The nose belonged to a large, normally placid lad, with whom words about something or other that was vitally important had been exchanged. This developed into a fight, or more specifically the boy, who was no match for David's pugilistic skills, began flailing about with his fists. Thanks to a previous encounter with a solid object, the flailer's nose pointed slightly to the left. David bided his time then hit it, which resulted in a horrible crunching noise, an agonised scream, the sound of blood spattering on tarmac and a bloodstained white gym kit. In due course the nose recovered but with a slightly rightward lean, just like the rest of Britain under Mrs Thatcher.

David's mother was Czech and had escaped to Britain in 1968, taking her son with her, and they'd wound up on a tough housing estate on the outskirts of Cambridge (yes, such places existed). We disliked each other almost on sight. He was streetwise and in many ways a lot more grown up than me, spoke with an appealing mixture of the obscenely profane and the articulate, and made friends quickly, mixing with the sort of people who thought I was a pain in the arse, a view with which he sensibly concurred. He was also good at thumping people, and I had no wish to be thumped.

His other weapon was charm. He was as averse to work as I was, but somehow could whittle away a teacher's irritability, whereas I just seemed to make them angrier, although some of them were given short shrift. They had few sanctions against us, and we knew it.

Things changed when David and I discovered a shared interest in antisocial behaviour, and I'm slightly ashamed to say that we bonded when I discovered that at the local supermarket it was possible to label the customers with a price gun without them noticing. My, how we laughed at that. It was like ringing birds. You'd see labelled people all over Letchworth.

We also discovered that it was possible to squeeze between the meat freezers, stand behind their fascias, wait for a hand to reach for a frozen joint, then take hold of it from under a fascia and have a frozen food tug of war. Why we were never caught I cannot imagine, but it did, I'm afraid, look very funny.

Which brings us back to the Mini. We'd extracted some scrap vehicle keys from a breaker's one boring Saturday afternoon, and discussed the idea of going to the staff car park in the small hours and moving all the cars about, then locking them up again afterwards.

We arrived after midnight. The moon was full, lighting everything and making us easy to spot. Driving the cars would be too noisy, moving them hard work. I tried the Mini's door with a key, and it opened. The car was light and easy to push. We wheeled it out of the car park, past the woodwork shed and onto the school field. There was the cricket pitch, a perfectly flat grass rectangle made grey by the moonlight. It looked like a giant postage stamp.

'Let's leave it there.'

Wheeling the little car into the middle of the square, we put it in gear, yanked up the handbrake, then locked it. For good measure we let the tyres down.

The shit hit the fan during the following morning's constitutional walk. The whole school trooped past the Mini as it squatted on the pitch. Finding it locked, the cricket First Eleven tried picking it up and carrying it away, but the car wouldn't budge.

During assembly one teacher announced with thunder in his voice, 'You will have seen the Mini on the cricket square. It was obviously put there by someone who is reasonably strong, has a passing interest in cars, AND HAS NEVER DONE A GOOD THING FOR THE SCHOOL IN HIS LIFE!'

'Martin!' whispered some of my classmates, inches from the back of my neck.

I denied everything, and was told by several cricketers, who were mostly members of the school's great and good, that they couldn't prove it was me yet, but when they did, they would fucking kill me. Well, that would teach the bastards for being so happy and successful, wouldn't it? And anyway it was just a laugh, wasn't it?

The groundsman who crank-started his Morris Minor van didn't think so, and resigned, which tempered the enthusiasm David and I felt for our prank, but eventually he was persuaded to stay, a process helped by the fact that letting down the tyres had spread the car's weight, leaving the pitch virtually undamaged. So that absolved us of any guilt for making this man's life a misery and nearly trashing what to him was a labour of love.

This sort of thing meant that when other bad stuff happened that had nothing to do with me, those in authority often decided I was probably involved and I would be hauled in for questioning. On other occasions a couple of staff of the 'I want to be your friend' variety, whom I trusted slightly less than they trusted me, would ask us to 'tell [them] about your problems.' One, who was little more than a boy himself and very naïve, usually started off by saying, 'For God's sake, if you've got any problems . . . .' His mirthless bridling when we began to imitate this phrase was very satisfying.

These encounters happened ad hoc in corridors, sometimes with other people around, sometimes not. I felt like a bug under a microscope, and rightly or wrongly, that these people wanted to know about me as an interesting case, the subject of a sociology exam, rather than as a person, and since the family stuff was private, talking about it to adults I didn't much like or respect seemed redundant.

The older one also had a bad reputation for being indiscreet. Have a 'private' conversation with this man and another teacher might suddenly ask you about something which had clearly stemmed from it. So I would say 'no thank you,' but these two would not be deflected. I was not cheered when the older one said to me:

'You can talk about your mother, but you don't have to. We've got it all on file.'

This was probably bullshit, but at the time I thought a private boarding school had no business holding stuff about Mum 'on file,' so clammed up completely. In the end I gave him the full teenage silent insolence treatment, and wouldn't even tell him what I'd been doing on my holidays. He didn't have much idea what I was doing at school either.

My first kiss involved a great deal of suction, a clash of enamel, and I think she'd been to the sweet shop because it was a bit gritty.

Two tall blonde Finnish girls had arrived for the summer term on some sort of student exchange, and possibly because English wasn't their first language I hadn't bored them into a coma ('You have picture of car on wall, yes?'). They liked boys, in the frank, practical way that some people enjoy food, and the taller of the two, who had a knowing look and a slight gap between her bottom front teeth, decided to amuse herself by whipping my teenage hormones into a spin cycle of lust. It rather took my mind off cars.

Until this point my experience with girls was that they didn't fancy me. Until recently most of them hadn't liked me either, but as I'd become acceptable company for some of the boys they did fancy, and we started to get to know each other as people, there was a bit of a reappraisal. So I was now on the periphery of the sometimes-adult, sometimes-childish passions, alliances, friendships, rows, betrayals and relationships that were both deeply important and entirely transient. Not a player, but a semi-detached observer. It was big improvement on what I was used to.

Although I had discovered a liking for Ian Dury, much of the music in my head was still of the noodling, uncool prog rock variety, but the people I was mixing with had different tastes. This was the era of 2 Tone records and the British ska revival, exemplified by Madness and The Specials, whose youthful energy and rage suited the era. At the time I thought I didn't like this stuff, but because it was good, it found its way into my head anyway and has stayed there ever since.

So in the summer of 1980 even I knew who Suggs was, but of course I also knew by then that the car which was supposedly going to replace the Mini and rescue the British motor industry would be christened the Metro, and had the code name 'ADO88'. This was because during one of my bottom set chemistry lessons, which were generally noisy battlegrounds of adult despair and fury and practised adolescent truculence and cheek, I'd propped my briefcase on my desk and hidden behind it as I read about the Metro in *Car* magazine, until the enraged teacher, a small long-haired person with blazing eyes and knitted sweaters that were always too big for him, plucked the magazine from my fingers and tore it to shreds. Good man.

I knew exactly what his feelings about me were, but having been an entirely flirtation-free zone was blithely unaware of what the Finnish girl thought until she'd more or less dragged me under the stairwell by the lapels. The world went dark, I saw stars and a tension that made me as brittle physically as I often still was verbally, ebbed and receded. I had no idea what to do next, so asked my friend David, who rolled his eyes.

'Go and see her after lights out.'

He then made a number of suggestions about what I should do once I'd arrived. As I was still painfully naïve, these came as a surprise.

So at 10.30 I sneaked into the school grounds, a frothing mass of innocence, ineptitude and intent. I was not a conventional male bimbo. I wore brown moccasin slippers that were half a size too big, so my feet kept flopping out of them, and orange Brentford Nylons pyjamas. Nylon from Brentford was a dangerous material in clothing. Walk quickly so that your knees rubbed together and the static electricity made your hair stand on end. This stylish ensemble was topped off with a pale blue towelling dressing gown, on which an MG car key fob insignia had been stitched. As 'M' and 'G' were my initials and had a car connection, the idea was that I might possibly hang on to the dressing gown if I knew that it definitely belonged to me.

In order to suck face in the dark I had to traverse the outside of the school grounds and re-enter through a creaking wooden door, up a creaky flight of wooden stairs, along a creaky wooden corridor at the end of which was an annex, where a member of staff would tick off everyone's names after they had been put to bed. Just before that was a flight of stairs that led to the room containing the Finnish girls.

I made it through the door and up the first flight of stairs, and saw the 'For God's Sake' man/boy teacher peering into a register. If I went downstairs he might hear, and since I was clearly in the wrong part of the school late at night, this would be awkward. Directly in front of me was a single loo. I walked purposefully across the corridor and went into it. The teacher did not look up as I shut the door and locked it.

The window was big enough to climb through, and next to it was a large green cast-iron drainpipe. This would make a very good escape route to the ground, which was about eighteen feet below. I flushed theatrically, slid back the loo door lock, clambered out of the window, scrambled down the drainpipe and skulked in the shadows until the upstairs lights went out. After fifteen minutes I went back through the doors and began climbing the stairs. Halfway up I froze, as coming up behind me was the sound of heavy, loud, booted footsteps.

BANG! BANG! BANG!

I turned and there was another boy. He was about six foot two, built like an isosceles triangle, and wearing blue Brentford Nylons pyjamas and Dr. Martens boots. He was also profoundly deaf. There's nothing funny about hearing loss, which can be extraordinarily isolating, and this boy was both academically very gifted and absolutely furious. He was probably going to be good-looking when he was finished, but he wasn't finished when I knew him, and instead was a teenager who wore bottle glasses and had the look of a Picasso painting, with features that had yet to coalesce into entirely the right places.

He was also equipped with the standard National Health Service hearing aid. These days digital aids are quite discreet, but in 1980 people with hearing loss were issued with a fag packet sized pink plastic box, allegedly flesh coloured, and filled with batteries, attached to a pair of pink wires and a couple of pink ear pieces (bad luck if you were black). These things weren't very good. Old ladies wore them on buses and whistled.

This lad was a thinker, and had decided that if he used his, those in authority would hear it whistling before they heard him, so he'd turned it off, which made him loud in other ways.

'WHO ARE YOU GOING TO SEE?!' he bellowed.

I had to repeat the name loudly several times.

He thought about it then roared 'PHWAAA!'

After that he shouted the name of his love interest then yelled, 'FOLLOW ME AND WE WON'T GET CAUGHT.'

'BANG! BANG! BANG!' went the boots as he smashed his way to the top of the darkened stairs, at which point a voice said. 'What are you doing?'

. It was 'For God's Sake.'

I ducked between them, flung myself back into the loo, locked the door, and waited to be told to come out. When that didn't happen I scrambled out of the window and grabbed at the drainpipe. My dressing gown had come undone and I did not get hold of the drainpipe as I would have wanted, instead hooking one hand round the back of it and planting one foot against the wall. My free hand and foot flapped wildly as I swung backwards and forwards like a giant orange and blue flag. A light had been turned on in the corridor beyond the loo, and I could see the teacher and his captive silhouetted through a pair of big open windows. Each time I swung into view I could hear words like 'expulsion' and 'the death penalty' (I made the last one up, but you get the gist). If the teacher turned round at the wrong moment, I would be perfectly illuminated. Instead I finally grabbed the drainpipe, shinned down it and scuttled back to bed frustrated, but not as frustrated as the enormous queue for the loo the following morning, because I'd forgotten to unlock the door.

I wasn't expelled, but I was asked not to come back. In fact, it was suggested to my father that he might like to take me away fourteen days before the end of term, when, after all, they'd had their money's worth – or belly full, depending on how you view these things. I resisted, in part because of the Finnish girl, with whom I was having occasional slobbering encounters, although I was not alone, discovering later that between them, she and her friend had six boys on the go, including a strutting Aryan proto-management consultant, who would have been horrified to discover that a person he regarded as a serial teenage dirt-bag and entirely beneath his contempt was his love rival. Now I rather admire those girls' industry, and have one memento from my very brief encounter with them, which I treasure. It's a record sleeve on which my amore had written 'THANK FOR WASHING POWDER.'

Academically, what I got from five years of private education was a furious, vicious school report, which had the words 'payback time' written all over it, and a CSE (Grade 2) in History. I'd been at that school for four-and-a-half years too long and it had been a painful, colossal waste of everyone's time.

Yet I felt oddly optimistic about my future, which had to be better than my present, and would, I felt certain, involve cars in some way. I wondered why nobody else seemed to agree.

# Four-Wheeled Dreams, Two-Wheeled Reality

The one-piece orange motorcycle suit was designed to keep heat in and the weather out, which was a mixed blessing.

Given that I was in the middle of a thunderstorm, with only my head and hands exposed, the waterproof element was a positive, although my hair was plastered down and soaked, and my hands had too-long-in-the-bath wrinkles, so that the bits of me that were visible had a tortoise-like quality. The heavy motorcycle boots I was wearing were also entirely rain resistant. The bad news was that I was riding a bicycle from Shepherds Bush to Harley Street, labouring up Holland Park Avenue towards Notting Hill Gate, having negotiated the lethal White City Roundabout, which in 1981 had not been fitted with traffic lights and had the quality of a giant vehicular blender filled with buses and taxis.

Inside the suit I was wearing nothing but socks and a pair of pants, but it was still sauna-like as I sweated and slithered around inside it, as my underpants did a credible g-string impression and the ferocious rainstorm chucked buckets of freezing water into my face.

I was eighteen and this was my first job. As many of my schoolmates prepared for university, I was earning £50 a week working as a cycle delivery boy for a West London optician, a position secured through the Job Centre of the local FE college where I'd spent the preceding year cobbling together a small collection of not-very-useful O Levels.

'Do you have your own bicycle?' asked the optician. I drew

his attention towards a tired-looking machine bequeathed by a cousin. 'You'll do. Don't tell our current boy. He's going on holiday and doesn't know we're making him redundant.'

The Brixton Riots, with their torched houses, shops and cars, were a very recent memory, and many of the shops near the optician's business in Shepherds Bush had fitted hefty steel roller shutters in case the rioting should spread westwards. There was a nervy sense that London was under siege.

So was the optician's business. It repaired spectacles for rival firms as well as selling glasses and testing people's eyes. Repairs took place in a basement lab and were presided over by a small, neck-less, white-haired German man in a white lab coat who called me 'arsehole.' Actually, it came out as 'azzhoool.'

'Azzhoool, sweep ze floor!'

'I need a cheez roll from zee bakers . . . Here is ze money, buy it for me now, Azzhoool!'

I was also trained to use a piece of equipment that cut little plastic discs into lens shapes, a process which required a lot of squinting and was doing my sight no good at all.

'Noo, noo, noo Azzhoool, you are fucking zis up!'

At the end of my first week the optician informed me that he was keeping my pay cheque 'as a bonus for when you leave.' Later, after a couple of other wage cheques bounced, he changed his mind and paid me the money. 'How kind,' I thought.

There was also a cadaverous, old and entirely bald consultant optician who drank and became belligerent and ever more aggressive as the day wore on. This lugubrious man's capacity to screw up prescriptions after liquid lunches helped create that feeling of being under siege. I also had to answer the phone, and had become good at fobbing off the hire purchase company that wanted to repossess the optician's Vauxhall Cavalier, but it was harder to deal with a phone call that went something like this:

'That man was drunk!'

'Surely not.'

'He was. He breathed on my daughter and the fumes gave her a headache. Now he's prescribed the wrong glasses and her eyes are in agony! What are you going to do about it?'

'Oh God,' said the optician when I told him about the conversation.

Generally I was glad to escape from this angst and dysfunction when, with a pair of old carrier bags filled with hundreds of pounds worth of glasses slung under the drop handlebars of my ratty, three-speed bike, I would complete an uninsured, circular trip that took in Notting Hill, Knightsbridge and Hammersmith. I dreamed of owning a Bristol 401, but the bike was all I had, and as long as I wasn't run over it was keeping me fit. Soon I had a particularly strong left wrist, thanks to the bike having a bent front fork. When riding I'd kicked the mudguard to stop it rattling, my foot had been caught in the front wheel, slammed into the fork and I'd been catapulted over the handlebars, landing in a tangled heap on the road. My foot hurt like hell though amazingly nothing was broken, but after that one fork had a mild foot-shaped kink, which was enough to make the bike crab so that it could only be made to go in a straight line by exerting extra pressure on the left handlebar, which was both wrist strengthening and exhausting.

Bits, such as pedals, snapped off the bike, thanks to the week it had spent at the bottom of a swimming pool after it had been nicked. This was why my cousin had given it to me.

Another pissed misdiagnosis by the consultant optician was why I was cycling to Harley Street. A woman had been given a pair of contact lenses with the magnifying qualities of wine bottle bottoms. This resulted in visual impairment and a cancelled holiday. She'd arrived in a fury to collect the replacements, while outside the heavens opened. As thunder rolled up and down the Goldhawk Road and lightning turned the heavy, vibrating air pinky-blue, the woman, bristling with justifiable rage, was told that her contacts were in the basement being tinted, and would be available 'soon.'

Then the optician pulled me to one side and hissed. 'No they're not, they're in Harley Street, and you've got to go and get them!'

As the heavens split once more and the rain gushed I asked about getting a taxi.

'No need,' said the optician. 'I have waterproof clothing.' It was then that he produced the motorcycle suit and boots.

As I clomped past the woman she gave me a pitying look.

'He's lying, isn't he?' she said simply. I nodded and fled, returning two hours later half-drowned, suffering from heat stroke and a couple of pounds lighter. The owner of the contact lenses, whose face had flushed a dark, angry red, snatched the box containing her contacts, paid and stamped into the deluge, never to return.

Not long after that I dared to take a holiday, and a 'temporary' replacement was brought in from the Job Centre, whom I had to show my delivery route. He was short, lantern-jawed and rode a child's bicycle, which was positively lethal on Central London roads. This character hadn't much to say, beyond his belief that the job was permanent. I tackled the optician about this, who said that my going on holiday was 'very inconvenient,' that he would have 'to think' about whether there would still be a job for me when I returned, and, by the way, did I want to be paid that week?

It was obvious that this man was a serial hirer and firer, and that I was just the latest in a long line of teenage work fodder, but I still had a job to do, which was to collect the specs that needed repairing and bring them back. I had now been given a pair of shoeboxes to go with my carrier bags to offer extra protection to their contents. The Notting Hill optician filled a shoebox and said, 'Be careful, one of those frames belongs to Petula Clark.'

Holland Park Avenue is long, straight and steep. I could get up a good speed cycling down it, and was enjoying going hell for leather when I noticed a knot of stationary traffic ahead. My brakes weren't up to much, and as I neared this obstruction, which comprised a gaggle of black cabs and a number 88 Routemaster bus, my palms began to sweat because there wasn't much room to stop. Then a very new, very shiny red Renault 5, driven by an expensive-looking blonde girl of the social species then known as a 'Sloane Ranger', emerged from a side street, filled the traffic gap I was juddering towards, and stopped. My closing speed was probably about 20mph, and I wasn't wearing protective clothing. Cycle helmets were virtually unheard of in 1981. It was no longer a question of whether I would hit her car, but how hard and where.

By now my feet were scraping along the tarmac. There was a small gap between the Renault and the Routemaster so I aimed for it. I saw the look of surprise on the girl's face as I shot past, saw her flinch as the carrier-bagged box with Petula Clarke's glasses struck her door mirror with a shattering bang. Then I was gone. Ahead was a small gap between cabs. I jinked through this, the road opened up and I sped away. Sheer weight of traffic meant that the Renault girl couldn't catch up with me, and I streaked back to the shop. Once there I emptied the smashed contents of the shoebox onto the German's desk.

'Jesus!' he said, stirring the wreckage with a finger. 'Zees are preeddy fucked.'

After three months, so was my first job. I returned from holiday to be told my services were no longer needed. A few unemployed weeks later I bumped into the German lab technician.

'Ah Azzhoool!' he bellowed warmly. 'Sings are a bit better in von vey since you haf left. Ze consultant optician, he went on holiday. No job when he got back, but ze bad news is zat ve still haf zat boy viz ze baby's bicycle, and he is vey, vey stoopid.'

'You ver an azzhoool, Azzhoool,' he said, patting me on the shoulder, 'but he is even verse zan you! Amazing eh? I vood not haf believed it. Zat azzhoool he is a fucking idiot!' And with that ringing endorsement, he marched away.

# Bag Man

It was early 1982 and I was once again on my way to the Job Centre. Back then it had plenty of custom, as unemployment had reached 3 million for the first time since the 1930s, the news was filled with factory closures and mass redundancies, and Michael Foot, the wild-haired old man who'd become leader of the Labour Party, claimed that every job was attracting 32 applicants.

So Job Centres, which were essentially government-run labour exchanges and part of a post-1945 state-run paternalism on which Margaret Thatcher and her Conservative government seemed less than keen, were high street perma presences like Woolworths and Rumbelows. Outside, Job Centres had unlovely strip-lit orange fascias, inside there were uncomfortable orange seats and rows of notice boards containing white postcards with handwritten job descriptions.

'Typist required,' 'Bus Conductor,' 'Milkman,' 'Telesales Representative wanted for dynamic refuse sack supply business. No previous experience necessary.'

I plucked out this card and shouldered my way past the tired-looking middle-aged blokes with nicotine stained fingers, New Romantics with big hair and fey self-consciousness, and young West Indian men who, when I'd started at boarding school in the mid 1970s, were getting stopped by the police in Mk2 Ford Cortinas, and were now probably having similar experiences in flashier Mk3s.

We were confronted by a row of desks behind which sat

pasty-looking civil servants. I presented my card to one of them, he phoned the business, I spoke briefly to a strident-sounding woman who was its co-owner, and was told to report for an interview at her offices near Baker Street.

'Good luck,' said the civil servant.

For the purposes of the interview I changed into my suit, another bequest from the cousin who'd given me his bicycle. He's a lovely man, one of the kindest people I know, and I was grateful for the bike and the suit, but it was made from a scratchy brown synthetic material and was oddly furry, which from a distance made its wearer appear fuzzy at the edges. Its big-lapelled, wing-collared and bell-bottomed cut had been the acme of fashion in 1978. It now looked horribly dated, but being entirely fashion unconscious I didn't care. I wore a tie with the contours of a flat fish, which my grandmother tut-tuttingly helped me to do up, and went to see the bin liner floggers. They turned out to be Adelphe, a feisty woman of 37, whose parents were Greek. Her partner Chris was quieter, 28, blonde and expensive-looking. I must have done something right because they offered me the job.

'Twenty-five quid a week plus commission,' said Adelphe, 'and no bullshit.'

After fourteen days of not selling a single sack I was faced with getting the sack myself if things didn't change. Until that point I'd been terrified of picking up the phone, stuttering and awkward when I did. Now, with the certainty of being let go fast approaching and with nothing to lose, I relaxed and sold 1,000 '20 gauge' sacks to a nunnery in Penge: 'Not only are these cheaper than conventional sacks, they have a rubber content so that they stretch rather than tear' (which actually meant they stretched before they tore).

This led to a reprieve, and to everyone's amazement I soon developed a posh voiced, foot in the door telephone technique that sold bin bags to children's homes, shipping lines, boarding schools and a strip club in Eltham. This had nothing to do with writing about cars, nothing to do with owning and driving them, which was beyond my means, but it seemed I had some persuasive skills and the ability to find and talk to the right people, and these would eventually become very useful.

This was very much clinging to the underbelly of the deregulated jobs market which Margaret Thatcher and her swivel-eyed employment minister Norman 'Chingford Skinhead' Tebbit were beginning to unleash. Despite being directly in the path of this Darwinian approach to economics, however, I wasn't immediately flattened by it. And as the weeks rolled by and I became an increasingly capable, if erratic telesales rep, I also became a little less lost than usual.

This could not be said of Mrs Thatcher's son Mark, whose name, when it appeared in newspaper gossip columns, was often preceded by the word 'playboy.' Another word that clung to him was 'arrogant' and he exuded a hard to love self-confidence, which is perhaps why, when he took part in the 1982 Paris-Dakar rally and apparently 'got lost,' this became the subject of much amused comment, especially after he and his team mates were discovered unhurt and marooned in the Sahara Desert with their Peugeot 504 saloon, whose back axle had been smashed. Although I had by now shrugged off the childish belief that cars were alive, I confess to feeling sorrier for the Peugeot than its driver. As for legitimately becoming a driver myself, it looked as if staying in paid employment might just make this happen.

'Save a bit of money, and if you can last at that job for three months I'll pay for some driving lessons, but you have to fund some of them from the money you've saved,' said my dad.

By this stage he had acquired a car to go with the Goldwing. It was a tiny Honda Z600 coupé. Today the few survivors are highly prized, but in 1982 an eight-year-old Z600 was just a slightly weird, cheap old car. Little bigger than an original Fiat 500, it had a beautifully engineered, motorcycle-like 600cc, two-cylinder, light alloy air-cooled engine driving the front wheels through a gearbox that didn't have synchromesh, which matched the speed of the engine with the speed of the gearbox cogs, to avoid a nasty clashing of teeth. This meant carefully judging the changes to avoid making loud crunching noises. The Z had tiny tombstone vinyl seats, a silly roof console with a useless swivelling map-reading light and a dashboard with a rev counter. Shaped like a duck egg and featuring a TV screen-shaped back window/hatch, Honda only sold the Z in violent orange, with the option of huge, curling black stripes down its sides. It was faster than it should have been, could be wound up to an alleged 80mph, had a habit of locking its wheels in the wet, and I loved it.

Dad had bought the thing from someone whose houseboat was moored near his still incomplete vessel. The Z came his way after one very high tide flooded the little car up to its door handles. Having paid £250 for its waterlogged remains, he rescued it using a hair dryer amongst other things, and for the first few weeks we sat on old newspapers as the seats dried out.

Japanese cars used to go rusty, and the Z's river dunking meant galloping rot. It had also been resprayed a horrid yellow, and as the rust holes appeared the paint flaked and fell off. When the exhaust rusted through my dad repaired it with an old bean can and a couple of Jubilee clips. I thought the idea of driving it would be fun, but he saw this coming.

'If you pass your test, there's one other proviso,' he said. I asked what he had in mind. 'You aren't borrowing my car.'

My work environment was often demented and now seems very antique. I sat in a poorly lit room at the top of what had once been a four-storey Georgian townhouse. At street level its frontage had become a greengrocer's, and we shared the rest of it with a firm of solicitors.

I shared that room with a passing show of people who were either en route to better things and slumming it for a bit, or whose lives were as rudderless as mine. Many of them would get fired, sometimes more than once. This happened to me three times. Our tools were three tired desks and chairs, a pile of elderly telephone directories and cream plastic phones with heavy handsets, curly wires that knotted up, and dials. No computers, no databases. When things were going well there would be constant noise, chatter, phones being dialled, handsets dropped onto their cradles. Quiet periods were hard to conceal.

'I'm not hearing anything!' Adelphe would yell from the office next door. 'Get your arses into gear!'

One of the frequently fired was a very un-fey New Romantic called Terry, who mixed his sect's uniform of androgynous per-oxide hair and a blusher-enhanced complexion with a street-wise, barrow boy swagger. He was obsessed with a band called Japan and its arch, clever lead singer David Sylvian, but only appeared to know one line from one song, which he would croon over and over again in between making conversations or making phone calls.

'I second that emotion.'

'It's cheaper if you buy 5,000 sacks. You get a discount.'

'I second that emotion.'

'Terry! Get your arse into gear!'

'Fu-u-u-ck off' (half whispered, half sung) 'I second that emotion.'

He was a devotee of 'Dial-A-Disc.' Britain's telephone network was still just under the control of the Post Office when I began my telesales odyssey, and if you dialled 16 you'd get 'Dial-A-Disc,' which played a small selection of pop songs on a loop down the phone, over and over again. These were interspersed with a jingle that went 'Music in yer ear 'ole Dial A Disc!'

Thus I first heard The Stranglers' 'Golden Brown', Laurie Anderson's pretentious-but-compulsive 'O Superman', Paul McCartney and Stevie Wonder's criminally naff 'Ebony and Ivory', using a small telephone earpiece that sucked all the dynamics out of the noises they were making. I even heard Japan's David Sylvian squeaking 'I second that emotion.'

Terry lasted longer than the girl with the puppy, which she was allowed to bring to work, where it quickly demonstrated that it wasn't house trained. They left soon afterwards. Then there was the young mother with the baby. He was tiny, smiled a lot and being very mobile, spent the days happily crawling round the office, little hands pad-padding on the threadbare carpet as he scooted over the stains left from our attempts to clean up the dog turds. One day he consumed a large quantity of Farley's Rusks, which seemed to give him a lot of energy. I was closing a big sale, 5,000 sacks to a children's home in Surrey, when junior shot under my desk, found my left foot and began prodding it.

This was a tad distracting, but as small fingers began poking at my sock I kept going. The sale was nearly closed, the commission would go towards my driving lessons fund. Then I noticed that something was being massaged into my sock, and that something was wet. Peering under the desk I saw a happy baby face smiling up at me as little hands mulched the congealed Farley's Rusk extract its owner had just regurgitated into the fibres of my sock.

'Would you mind if I called you back in a moment?'

At about this time a small news item about a bunch of Argentinian scrap dealers landing on the South Atlantic island of South

Georgia and raising their national flag exploded when the Argentinian army invaded the Falklands themselves. The first I knew of this was when I saw the blaring *Evening Standard* news-stand hoardings outside Baker Street station announcing what had happened. I was nineteen, national service, which finished in 1960, was a recent memory for many, and there were plenty of people who thought bringing it back would be a good idea. If Britain went to war, many of my friends and I feared being conscripted.

'They're not putting me in the army,' said Terry. 'No way. I'd scarper first.'

I was learning to drive in a well-travelled Mk2 Ford Escort belonging to the Olympia School of Motoring, chosen because it had an ancient 1950s mock-up of a traffic light in its shop window that had been there for as long as I could remember. The driving school's instructors had apparently taught members of the exiled Greek Royal Family to drive, so it was good enough for me.

The Escort's clutch was vicious, engaging with the progressiveness of a light switch, which made my first encounter with it a jerk-filled experience. Its steering was alarmingly vague, with the precision of custard being stirred with a spoon. My instructor, a roguishly charming man in his thirties, had once driven lorries for Edwin Shirley Trucking, which painted its vehicles lurid purple and specialised in shifting equipment for rock concerts. I mentioned the car's uncommunicative steering and he smiled nostalgically.

'I like a bit of slop,' he said. 'It reminds me of the trucks.'

The Escort had dual controls, so the instructor could stop the car from the passenger seat. I gave him one or two scares, but he never felt the need to use them when I was at the wheel.

'You're better than one of my clients,' he said. 'She's very intense and we're always drifting towards parked cars, but if I try to dip the clutch or use the brake, she hooks her left foot under hers and keeps going.'

As I practised reversing round corners in grim White City housing estates, a Naval taskforce started the 5,000-mile journey from Portsmouth to the Falklands, where, once it arrived, a full-scale battle was soon underway. In a world where 'personal communications' involved stamps and domestic telephones, where the internet and mobile phones with cameras were the stuff of 'Tomorrow's World,' we learned about the awful ebb and flow of air strikes, battleships being sunk, and men dying through newspaper correspondents, reporters from the BBC and ITN, and daily bulletins from an official spokesman called Ian McDonald. A middle-aged man in a suit and thick-rimmed glasses who always refused to take questions, McDonald read out a list of often momentous happenings with an emotionless precision that earned him the nickname 'Ian McDalek.'

The tabloid press covered the story with a mix of patriotism and jingoism ('Gotcha' yelled *The Sun*'s headline when the Argentinian battle cruiser ARA *General Belgrano* was torpedoed). *Private Eye* lampooned the more febrile press coverage with the spoof headline 'Kill an Argy – and win a Metro,' but as the conflict progressed and it became clear Britain was going to win, it chimed in with how a lot of people felt.

As British forces re-claimed Port Stanley, the Falkland Island's capital, I, Terry and a generation of naïve young men shelved thoughts of being forced into Britain's professional army, whose chiefs must have shuddered at the prospect. So we weren't going to be shot at by South American soldiers, many of whom actually were conscripts. Instead I prepared to take my driving test, mugging up on the Highway Code and the intricacies of mirror use and hand signals in a way I'd never done with exams at school.

Whilst all this was going on I, or rather my dad, bought a car for £65. It was a 1956 Heinkel Kabine, in other words a three-wheeled bubble car, with a 174cc one-cylinder motorcycle engine driving its single rear wheel, and one door at the front of the vehicle, which just about had room for three people on its single bench seat. That it was left-hand drive hardly mattered, given how small the thing was. Instead of an ignition key it came with a tiny metal obelisk that was pushed into a slot, a couple of dashboard warning lights would glow dimly, you'd press the accelerator pedal, push a little button, and the engine would chuggingly turn over then fart into clattery life. Contrary to urban myth, the Heinkel had a reverse gear, which, like its four forward speeds, was accessed by a lever that could be pushed or pulled for gear selection purposes, and used a vague and floppy selection of rods to do this. Since only the handbrake worked, this was academic, as the Heinkel couldn't be driven. My dad allowed this egg-shaped car to camp in a corner of the small garden of his houseboat's moorings.

'I'll offer advice, but I'm not fixing it for you,' he said. 'That's your job, and if you ignore it, the car goes.'

So as I waited for my call-up papers, I spent a lot of leisure time stripping out the car's front suspension, cleaning and rust proofing its underside and putting everything back together, and rewiring it, a process that involved a lot of detective work with a length of wire, a torch bulb and a battery. This was hardly further education, but the car was improving, which was a confidence booster, and I was starting to learn how to learn.

Adelphe and Chris had met working for another bin bag telesales operation, and decided that they could do better on their own. Adelphe was the driving force. She mothered, nurtured and, with a temper that would have been the envy of a Wagnerian witch, terrorised when it suited her.

'What the fuck are you fucking doing?! I don't want excuses. No. FUCK excuses. You can do it! You can do it! I know you can fucking do it, so don't give me fucking bullshit!'

I couldn't do it with World Cup 1982 Bulldog Bobby carrier bags. Featuring a frankly crap England football team mascot, the ones we had were more expensive than those being sold in the corner shops that were our target market. So I nearly starved to death and was briefly sacked when we couldn't get rid of them, only to be asked back because I was still better than anybody else who came from the Job Centre.

I was making one of these fruitless sales calls when there was a dull, window-rattling concussion. It sounded far off but enormous, and was followed by the noise of emergency vehicle bells and sirens. This was the Hyde Park bomb, which took the lives of seven cavalry horses and eleven servicemen, a few weeks after the Falklands conflict had ended. The risk of being maimed or killed by an IRA bomb was something Londoners had grown used to living with.

Adelphe's husband, a bubble-permed Jeff Lynne lookalike, who appropriately worked as a rock concert caterer, might well have fed my driving instructor, and had a lively relationship with his wife. He was on tour in the States, and would reverse the charges so that they could have Transatlantic rows at her expense – there were no mobile phones for instant access to long distance domestic discord. She was also in regular contact with her mother and a tribe of aunts, who lived in North London but did not speak English. The phone would ring and a gravelly female voice would ask for Adelphe, and say 'Mother,' or 'Aunty' for identification purposes.

Chris's boyfriend, whom I never actually met, was an Arab arms dealer with the voice of Omar Sharif, perfect telephone manners and a lot of money.

'Good afternoon,' he would intone. 'Might I speak to Chris please?'

It wasn't thanks to bin bag sales that she drove a brand new VW Golf convertible, which almost never had the roof down 'because people will look at me.' She also drove her partner's left-hand drive BMW 6 Series coupé, one of the prettier cars from the 1970s. She punted this big shark-nosed machine through the tight London streets with great authority. When I pedalled home on my wonky bicycle at the end of the working day I would enviously watch her swish into the traffic, thinking that she was only a few years older than I was. Adelphe drove a battle-scarred, decade-old Fiat 124 had a cardboard box contours, which she frequently forgot to tax. I did not covet that in quite the same way.

This wealth gap, the gulf between the BMW and my push-bike, would in a wider sense become more and more evident as the 1980s wore on.

When I took my driving test in Hounslow, the acme of West London suburbia, it was with a sense of extreme anxiety. I was, my instructor reckoned, ready, but still over-zealous with my emergency stops.

'You keep locking the wheels, and they'll fail you for that,' he'd warned.

I also knew that Hounslow was where Elvi, my friend Jamie's actress mother, had last attempted to pass her driving test.

'We were on Hounslow High Street and doing quite well when a chicken shot across the road in front of the car,' said Elvi. 'I said, "I'm not going to ask you why it's doing that," the man with the clipboard looked very cross and failed me.'

The examiner who climbed into the car with me was about fifty. He wore a trench coat and an expression of funereal seriousness. He also had the voice of Ian McDalek.

'In your own time, pull away from the kerb please. In fifty yards I want you to turn right. Turn left at the next junction please. Exterminate.'

The emergency stop was one of the first things we did. The examiner banged his clipboard on the dash in the approved manner, and I banged on the brakes, briefly but obviously locking the wheels.

'That's torn it,' I thought, and relaxed. It was now a case of trying to get everything else right, then having another go. The pressure was off and I could concentrate properly. So I did the choreographed, theatrical mirror/signal/manoeuvre head and eye movements to show the man I was on the case, did that learner driver shuffling steering wheel thing that I'd no intention of continuing when I started driving, and reversed round a corner without bumping over the pavement.

'Park the car please.'

Out came the flip chart of road signs, which I'd looked at over and over again. I couldn't remember them all, but the ones that randomly flipped into view were familiar. Things had gone rather well, I thought. What a pity about the emergency stop.

The examiner was speaking.

'. . . pleased to say that you've passed your driving test.'

It took a few seconds to sink in. 'Really?' I was amazed. Feelings of uncomplicated pleasure washed through me. This was the first time I'd properly worked towards an exam, and I'd passed it at the first attempt.

'Well done,' said the examiner, as a tight, mechanical smile broke through his facial granite then retreated into impassivity.

It was Adelphe's birthday.

'Fuck it,' she said. 'Let's go for a meal.' We abandoned the phones, trooped into a basement restaurant, and spent an increasingly badly behaved afternoon getting drunk.

'Excuse me. Excuse me,' she said to a trio of dark-suited businessmen, who were trying to have a working lunch.

'Yes?'

'Why are you all so fucking boring?'

'Why not?'

'Now, now, come on. That doesn't answer the question!'

'Why are you so fucking rude?' That question was asked rhetorically.

'It's my fucking birthday.'

'Well, we'd better come and celebrate it with you then.'

So that's what they did, quickly becoming as drunk and daft as we were. Not long before we staggered up the restaurant stairs and onto the street, blinking in the sunlight, Adelphe asked me

'How big's your neck?

'What?'

'How big?' she said, made a strangling gesture with her hands then found her handbag, rummaged in it and pulled out a small paper bag, in which was a very simple silver necklace.

'A bloke can wear this,' she said. 'I bought it for me but it's too small. You're just a boy. Come here!'

She pulled me towards her, then clipped the necklace round my neck. It fitted very well.

'Present!' she said. 'It almost makes you look like a grown-up.'

A month later she gave me the sack for the third and final time. I'd run out of leads and run out of enthusiasm. I lacked the relentless, killer instinct that makes flogging stuff over the telephone bearable, and had got into hot water after ringing the owner of an old people's home and spending ten minutes commiserating with the man, who was close to tears, because his business had gone bust after twenty years, and the only person he could talk to about it to was a teenager trying to sell him rubbish bags.

'Yeah, yeah, yeah,' said Adelphe, who was a lot nicer than she made out. 'I'm not paying you to be Mr Social Services. We'll go bust if you don't get your arse into gear.'

It was soon obvious that my arse had selected neutral. 'I don't want to do this, because when you're good, fearless, you'll talk to anyone. But then you get lazy. Why are you lazy when you could be so good? I thought we could really make something of you, but it wasn't to be. I love you but you've got to go,' said Adelphe, adding cryptically, 'now fuck off and keep in touch.'

Which, like a great many of the oddballs and misfits she hired and fired, is what I did.

Instead of cycling straight home I pedalled to the nearest Job Centre, which was on Oxford Street. A fruitless half-hour later and I was back on the bike, crossing Oxford Street itself, and had reached the other side when I was engulfed by a shoal of pedestrians.

'Oi!' one of them shouted as we nearly collided. The voice sounded familiar.

'Gurdon!'

I turned and saw David, my Mini-moving compatriot from school. When last heard of he'd been living in a series of Cambridge bedsits; his serial moving about meant that we'd since lost touch.

'What the bloody hell are you doing here?' I asked.

David grinned. 'I've moved to London, and my girlfriend works in there,' he gestured at Selfridges. 'I'm just going to meet her. What are you doing?'

'Nothing. I've just been sacked.'

'Serves you right for nearly running me over. Suppose you'd better come too then.'

As bad days go, this had turned out to be rather a good one.

# Little Mouse, Big Break

'You don't want this job. It will bore you stiff.'

I was sitting in a very basic little office with an avuncular, round man in his sixties with a shiny bald pate and a tight dark blue suit that was entirely filled by his ample frame. Big hands folded over his big stomach, he rocked back in his chair, and looked at me thoughtfully.

'So why do you want to work here?'

'I need a job, and I'll work hard.'

I meant it. Weeks of penurious mooching about in my grandmother's house had frayed her nerves and mine.

I was often so broke that finding the bus fare to visit and work on the bubble car was beyond me.

'For goodness sake, darling, can't you find something to do?' asked my exasperated gran.

By then in her late eighties, she had reluctantly let me into her home on a permanent basis. My father, the youngest of her three sons, and still her baby, was different. She was delighted to have him around, especially as the work on the houseboat was taking far longer than expected.

In her sixties she'd looked after my four paternal cousins when their parents were working abroad; now older and frailer, she was reluctant to repeat the experience. I broke and fiddled with things, answered back, ate vast quantities and flopped around in her small scruffy sitting room when she would far rather have had it to herself.

The bicycle and suit cousin was living in the first floor flat, her sister Joan, and a demented Yorkshire terrier called Susie that she'd not long acquired, remained in her bedsit flat, and the elderly Polish tenants seemed to have gone completely bonkers.

What ghastly experience had brought them to London was never explained to me, but it was probable they'd been refugees from the last war. Their flat was filthy and needed redecorating. My uncle had offered to put them up in a bed and breakfast while it was cleaned and painted, but they weren't budging, and there had been explosions of rage from the husband.

'This is lies! All lies! You must think I am stupid. You will take the flat and give it to someone who will pay more, and we cannot pay more, so we will not move!'

He'd then taken to accusing my 86-year-old grandmother of being a spy.

'You have transmitter in the cellar! I have seen it, I have heard it. You are spy for the Russians!'

My grandmother's cellar actually contained decades' worth of junk and dust-covered bottles of elderflower wine, which she had made years before. On occasion these would explode loudly, spraying yellowed newspapers and old suitcases with sugary shards of glass.

'Why don't we drink some of it?' asked my dad.

'It's not ready yet,' said my grandmother.

She had all this to contend with, and a heart condition, so adding me to the mix didn't fill her with joy, but just like Aunt Pat and Uncle Mick, she let me into her home.

I had tried to get work, having recently failed to become a toilet roll stacker or to chauffeur synth pop duo Yazoo in a Ford Fiesta, which was one of the more unusual employment opportunities offered by Hammersmith Job Centre. Given that I hadn't driven a car since taking my test it was perhaps just as well that I didn't get that, as one mistake could have ended the subsequent careers of Alison Moyet and Erasure, the band her musical partner Vince Clarke formed after they'd split up, which would have been tragic – at least in one case.

The job I was applying for when I met the big man in the suit involved working as a foot messenger for the photo dispatch department of Press Association news agency, delivering black and white prints of news photographs into the offices of all the national newspapers, then still grouped in and around Fleet Street. Thanks to the internet and digital photography, this work is now as antique and redundant as the hot metal typesetting still being used by newspapers in 1982 when I applied for the job.

I gave my interviewer my best spaniel-eyed look, he took pity and reluctantly gave me the job. I had wanted to be a journalist, and would now be amongst the biggest concentration of journalists in the country, but not writing a word, and would go from a very female-dominated working environment to a hierarchical, blokey one.

The job was based in a busy, strip-lit area that didn't have much in the way of natural light. There was a room containing people who typed captions that were stuck on the back of the prints, taken by a roster of photographers. This being the era of 35mm film, there was also a darkroom from which these prints emerged, to be sorted and placed in black rectangular hessian sacks with the names of the newspapers on them. Different papers wanted different pictures, so these were collated, and the messenger 'boys', who actually ranged in age from seventeen to about seventy, were given different rounds, which took us to the newspaper picture desks where we'd hand over the photographs. With the exception of one caption writer, everybody there was male, some had grown up with each other and quite a few were related. There were two brothers from Bermondsey. One, about my age, delivered photographs, but had designs on promotion into the darkroom where his elder brother already worked. Their dad, softly spoken and Irish, was a security guard. The place smelled of chemicals and tobacco, and yes, the work was intensely boring.

This was because we spent most of the time sitting on vinyl chairs facing each other in a little anteroom, often spending hours waiting for the pictures which we would then trudge round the editorial offices delivering. Tabloid newspapers would be read, conversation exchanged, laddish ones amongst the younger messengers, 'the world's going to the dogs' ones from the two old boys, John and Ivor. John was flat-hatted, seventy, tiny, spare, deaf and short of breath. Sometimes he struggled round the delivery routes, but was absolutely resistant to the idea of retirement. Ivor, fat and in his late sixties, wore faded jackets and ties, spoke with a gently pompous subservience and called everybody 'Sir.'

John read the racing pages and would mumble in wet-lipped, false-toothed bursts that were sometimes hard to understand.

'Just agree with him,' said the boy from Bermondsey.

Ivor sat Buddha-like and immobile, before suddenly expostulating mid thought, verbalising half of what was in his head, so that out of context it made no sense.

'Mrs Thatcher, Sir. Great lady, great lady,' he'd say, then fall silent again. Sometimes he would fix you with a piercing look and ask a question about something for which he clearly felt there was a right answer.

'Sir Robin Day, Sir. A great man, do you not think?'

This sometimes led to low-level teasing.

'Who's that, Ivor?'

Ivor would shake his head in disgust and mutter, 'Shame on you, Sir. Shame on you.'

Both he and John had a habit of falling asleep, heads back, mouths open, snoring lustily. We found this endlessly funny. The job involved inaction, repetition and tedium, but these two old men clung to it fiercely.

My shift started at midday and ended at six in the evening, which technically left the morning free to pursue other interests, but a mixture of torpor and a practised ability to avoid anything I might not be able to do meant that I sank into a melancholic immobility.

I'm not sure what made me visit *Car* magazine's headquarters during a lunch break. At the time it was based in offices over a bank in Smithfield, opposite the meat market, a ten-minute walk from the Press Association.

I went up in a rattly old lift, knocked on the door, had a short 'Can I help you?' conversation with someone, who, on being told that I wanted to be a motoring journalist, said something along the lines of 'That's nice. The editor's out. I think you should write to him.'

Three minutes later I was back on the street. I nearly didn't write that letter, assuming that it was a waste of time, but in the end decided that if I was going to it would be best to suggest some story ideas. I laboriously handwrote the letter and persuaded my grandmother to check the spelling. 'No darling, "their", not "there."'

A week after it was posted I came back from work to be told someone called Steve Cropley had phoned.

'He edits that magazine you wrote to,' said my grandmother. 'He wants to talk to you. Is he Australian? He seems very nice.'

This was the man who'd taken over from Mel Nichols as *Car*'s editor. When I rang him my hands shook.

'How old are you?' said Steve Cropley.

'Nineteen.'

'I'm very old,' he said. 'I'm 33.'

I thought 'Yes you are,' but decided not to say so.

He wanted to know if I'd ever been published, asked one or

two car-related questions, then said 'What do you know about the man who designed the original Fiat 500, the Topolino, you know, the one from the 1930s?'

Oh God, I couldn't remember his name, but did know that he'd been in charge of designing Fiats up to a boxy little saloon called the 128, which was cleverer than it looked, giving 80 per cent of its space to passengers and their luggage – it was, fascinatingly, 1970's Car of the Year. I'd read about this in an old copy of *Car*, quite possibly in a science lesson at school. Suddenly this had become useful information.

'Well,' said Cropley. 'You do know who this man is, and he's called Dante Giacosa by the way, you showed some initiative coming to see us and your letter is articulate. I don't think much of the ideas, but how would you like to write 1,000 words on the Fiat Topolino?'

Speechless with excitement, I made an affirmative mumbling noise.

'Thank you,' said Cropley, as if I was doing him a favour. 'I'd like the story in a week.'

I wrote and researched my 1,000 words in a vacuum of complete ignorance, but oddly the year I'd spent ringing up strangers and flogging them plastic bags came in useful. I'd learned how to pick up a telephone, get through to the right people and persuade them to talk to me. I unearthed a Fiat owners' club, whose membership contained a Topolino expert. As with so many car fans I discovered that he loved talking, and what he told me about the design quirks of the car, and some of the social history surrounding it gave me 80 per cent of the information I needed.

I'd discovered a bookshop whose basement was filled with stacks of aged motoring magazines, visited it and worked my way through copies until I found a couple of period road tests and some other Topolino-related stuff which backed up and expanded on what I'd been told. Then I wrote my first article, by hand, in an old exercise book.

'Finished,' I told my dad. It was, I felt, pretty bloody good.

He read it, then handed it back.

'Read it again,' he said. 'Aloud.'

This wasn't what I wanted to hear. I'd worked hard on my 1,000 words, and couldn't see why it needed looking at again.

'Go on,' he said. 'Read it aloud.'

Oh dear. By my own lips every punctuation error was tripped over, every clunking simile exposed. There was also the order of information, or more specifically, the fact that all the information was there, but spattered about so that it jumped backwards and forward by decades as important details had come to mind and I'd crowbarred them in to the text in no particular order. Word processors, which offered the luxury of taking bits of information and shoving them about until they were all in the right place, barely existed, and my butterfly brain wasn't used to being made to think in a linear way.

'What do you need to do now?'

'Write it again.' God, I was pissed off, but it couldn't be avoided.

I rewrote that bloody piece about fifteen times, by hand, at home in the mornings, on the train to work, at work, on the train home again, and late into the evening. Then my dad, who often returned at eight or nine at night, would sit down with me and we would go over what I'd done, sentence by sentence, line by line.

'I didn't know what I was doing,' he said years later, 'but I could tell when something was wrong, and knew when it felt right.'

The final draft was the right length, had its chronology sorted, and was a workmanlike, clean piece of writing. A girl who was a secretary in the office below my former bin liner employers ('Martin! How are you, you lazy bastard?') typed this journalistic monolith, which I dropped off at *Car*'s offices, and waited in pleasurable agony to hear how it had been received.

'It's good,' said Steve Cropley. 'We'll use it in about three issues' time. By the way, we'll pay you £150.' This was pretty much what I earned in three weeks.

So this was how I made my publishing debut, on a single page, at the back of *Car*. Can you imagine how excited I was? How relieved, how insufferable? I was officially a car expert.

'How many wheel nuts has that Fiat got, then?' asked my dad's friend Ken. He knew teenage bullshit when he met it. I didn't know much, but I did know how to find out about stuff, and what I'd done was an indication that I might not, after all, spend the rest of my working life in dead end jobs, that I might perhaps have some talent as a writer, and that a lack of qualifications and mixed-ability social skills might not prevent it from being realised. This was a fantastic opportunity, unless I screwed it up.

So I screwed it up, which even then I somehow knew I would. Not having the faintest idea about the work and stresses involved in putting together a magazine month after month, and with a desperate wish to escape the messengering job, which was boring me senseless, I pestered and eventually irritated, and did not work for *Car* again, which at the time was the source of childish anguish and extreme frustration, but in the longer term turned out to have been a very good thing.

The *Daily Express* and *Evening Standard* operated from an elegant art deco building known by some as 'the Black Lubyanka.' Its lobby was a riot of polished metal, exotic curves and marble floors, but inside the corridors had the feel of Meccano, with metal walls, ceilings and floors, on which your shoes clanged. The big open-plan editorial floors were typical of much of Fleet Street at the time. They were mostly filled with chain-smoking blokes typing, usually with two fingers, on hefty Adler manual typewriters, whose chimes and clattering filled these spaces with noise.

A visit to *The Sun* and the *News of the World*'s offices involved getting lifts that had minds of their own; press the second floor button and the lift might take you to the floor above or the basement, where hot-metal compositors worked on huge ancient typesetting machines and the place rumbled and vibrated with the sound of printing presses. Once a man in a suit got into the lift with me, pressed the third floor button and the lift instantly took him there.

'That's unusual,' I said.

'Not for me it isn't', said Sir Nicholas Lloyd. 'I edit the *News of the World*.'

By 1983 probably the most famous female columnist was Jean Rook of the *Daily Express*, who proudly styled herself 'the Bitch of Fleet Street.' Tall, chain-smoking, of indeterminate middle age, she had a sort of hard-edged glamour that was vaguely 1940s Hollywood leading lady, and her own office, which I passed several times a day, catching a glimpse of her spectral outline in the swirling fog of fag smoke. She sat at an imposing desk with her back to a large window overlooking Fleet Street, so often all I could see was the outline of big hair and shoulders encased in furs.

After my publishing debut infrequent commissions had followed, enough to scrape together some cuttings, which led to a job interview as a reporter for *Autocar* magazine. I met the editor on a Tuesday. 'I think I'm going to take you on,' he said. 'I'll let you know by the end of the week.' Two weeks later and I was still waiting, but didn't dare ring about 'my' job. Instead I decided to show some initiative and write something on spec for the magazine. *Autocar* had a weekly 'celebrities with cars' slot, and the only famous person I could get anywhere near was Jean Rook. Fearful that this could result in trouble with the Press Association if Rook complained, I asked her secretary if she would talk to me, explaining that the story was on spec and might never be published.

'I'll ask,' she said. A week later the secretary beckoned me over and said that her boss had agreed.

As I sat on a chair that was quite a lot lower than hers, I thought that Rook had the air of a benign vulture. She owned a Rover 3500, explaining raspingly that she didn't like 'girly' cars. She might have been 'the Bitch of Fleet Street,' but she was kind to me: prompting questions, and providing funny, in character quotes. She was my very first interviewee, and made sure that the piece virtually wrote itself.

I dropped off the copy at *Autocar*'s office, and the next day the phone rang. Another interview they'd lined up had fallen through, they were desperate for a replacement, and when could Jean Rook be photographed? She was just as obliging to them and a week later I was in print.

I did not become *Autocar*'s reporter, thanks to Alexei Sayle, who'd used the F-word in his 'celebrity with a car' interview. I'm told this resulted in the editor being relieved of his post three days after his verbal job offer to me, which looking back was a blessing, as I wasn't ready, and probably would have been fired.

Instead I freelanced for the magazine, mostly writing more 'famous people and their cars' stories, learning my craft and getting paid to interview the likes of Alan Coren and film critic Barry Norman.

I was so broke and scruffy-looking that Norman took pity and insisted on buying me a drink and a sandwich. Coren liked cars. He was still editing *Punch* magazine, and the photographer and I met him after one of its famous *Punch* lunches. He was feeling no pain at all, and gave us a hilarious two hours of freewheeling, discursive thought, so we were completely immersed in word-play and intelligence. This encounter had the quality of taking a bath: complete immersion in wit. We laughed so much that afterwards it hurt to breathe. This did wonders for my endorphins, and made a Technicolor contrast to the depressing grey slog of my day job.

Coren talked about flattening his Austin Healey 3000's exhaust on some cobbles in Italy, expecting local mechanics to be able to fix it 'with a piece of pasta, but in fact they were all useless.' He also described a Morris Oxford with a peculiar automatic transmission which broke, so the Sage of Cricklewood fixed it. 'Of course no other car had that transmission, so I learned a lot of pointless things about Morris Oxford automatics.'

Taking a long, pleasurable drag from an umpteenth cigarette, Coren said, 'Do you know, Benny Green, our jazz critic, doesn't drive? That's like saying that you don't fuck.' Mindful of Alexei Sayle, we left that bit out.

By now I could type, having been given a very old Pitman's manual by a friend's mother, and the use of an ancient manual typewriter by my grandmother. This hefty object's keys would stick and its ribbon tied itself in knots, but I would drag it to the Press Association, sit in a corner and hammer out occasional writing commissions, then slog round Fleet Street delivering photographs. During the prolonged, vicious miners' strike of 1984, I arrived with a photo of the miner's union leader, Arthur Scargill, at *The Sun*'s picture desk, knowing it would get their interest. A po-faced, beanie-hatted Scargill was seen on a march with one arm raised, looking as if he was at a 1930s Nuremberg Rally.

'Look at this!' cried the picture editor, as Kelvin McKenzie and company crowded round.

That evening the BBC News announced that production of *The Sun* had been suspended after the print unions had objected to the front page. There was 'my' picture of Scargill and the headline 'Mine Führer.'

Although I hated the Press Association's monotony, the sense of being becalmed, and the 'keep your head down and don't rock the boat' feel of the place, these were some of the best work colleagues I've ever had. I didn't fit into their world at all, but was never bullied, never discouraged. They probably thought I was barking mad, but didn't say so. This conformist place was surprisingly benign and tolerant, which is why Ivor's habit of muttering to himself while fishing old newspapers out of litter bins and collecting them in plastic bags to take home, or turning up and sitting in the anteroom over the Christmas holidays rather than face his wife, were tolerated just as much as my attempts at writing about cars.

I began to build up a file of cuttings, including the occasional car-related feature for *Options*, a women's magazine edited by Sally O'Sullivan, who'd married *Times* editor Charles Wilson after he'd unhitched himself from Anne Robinson.

The frothy, showy 1980s had created young upwardly mobile professionals who'd been given the unflattering sobriquet of 'yuppies'. They all seemed to drive Volkswagen Golf GTIs, many painted white, stripped of all chrome work and coated in matching plastic aerofoils and wheel extensions. Made by German firms with names like Kamei, BBS and Neuspeed, some of these looked good, but others gross and hilarious, like vac-formed warts. I cold-called O'Sullivan from a payphone, spoon-feeding it 10 pence pieces, and offered to write about this trend. She, very much a glossy magazine industry grandee, agreed.

This meant that instead of writing for car enthusiasts, who would know that a 'spoiler' was something that improved the way a car cleaved the air rather than ruined its looks, I was writing for an intelligent lay audience who didn't, and almost certainly didn't care. My work was edited by some very talented people, who wanted to read something that was accurate, fun and understandable. Without realising it, I learned an enormous amount from them, and much of what I learned still goes into my work now.

Being a news agency, the Press Association had a floor filled with journalists, cranking out news stories that could be sold elsewhere, and one of them, who wrote about motorsports on the side, heard about my infrequent forays into print.

'The desk editor likes cars. Bring a couple of cuttings and I'll introduce you,' he said.

So one frantically busy afternoon I appeared with a dog-eared scrapbook containing my Fiat Topolino article, a couple of things I'd written for a petrol station giveaway newspaper called *The London Motorist*, Jean Rook, Barry Norman, Alan Coren and the *Options* feature.

The desk editor was a fierce-looking Geordie called Mike Imeson, who was not pleased to be introduced to a teenage wannabe motoring hack who spent his days delivering photographs for £54 a week.

Without looking at the scrapbook he snapped.

'He wants to be a journalist? Really? Whose going to want his stuff? Look son, I haven't got time for this. You're up against people who've been to university and have degrees in engineering.'

With that he stomped off. My motorsport friend told me not to worry. 'He's just having a bad day, and his bark's worse than his bite. Leave the cuttings and I'll get him to look at them.'

Later, I was back on the editorial floor when the scary Mr Imeson fixed me with a steely gaze.

'I hadn't realised that you'd been published. And actually, your stuff is quite good. If I'm not too busy I'll check it over before you send it if you'd like.'

So before anyone else saw my efforts, they'd been under the blue pencil of a vastly experienced Fleet Street desk editor, who despite heart attack workloads was never too busy to clean up 500 Tippex-encrusted words on *Doctor Who* actor Peter Davison's Ford Sierra 4x4 or a piece about the Scootacar, a plastic bubble car briefly produced by a railway carriage maker in Hunslett, Yorkshire.

'What's this?' Mike would rasp at some grammatical cock-up, or 'you really don't get apostrophes, do you?' but the man's enormous kindness was ill concealed.

It took another eighteen months before I escaped the messengering job, passing through smoke-filled editorial offices and sharing space with the likes of Keith Waterhouse, Marge Proops and the jolly, scary Anne Robinson (or should that be 'jolly scary?').

To become a motoring journalist I knew I'd have to escape from the cradle of British journalism, which in the mid-1980s, just before Rupert Murdoch shipped out to Wapping, had an exciting, seedy decadence that felt as if it was about to come apart at the seams, which it duly did.

I spent a year buying the *UK Press Gazette*, applying and failing to get a series of reporting and copywriting jobs, but eventually a public relations agency specialising in motoring took a deep breath and offered me a job.

On my last day at the Press Association, I passed Jean Rook's office and saw the wraith-like outline of the columnist, chain-smoking behind her huge desk. After our interview I never spoke to her again, but her secretary smiled and waved to me as I trudged by.

'Good luck,' she mouthed.

# The 5p Car

My dad was insistent.

'Give me five pence,' he said.

Since it was my birthday, this seemed like a strange request, but I rummaged in my wallet and handed over a coin.

'Ok,' said my dad. 'This is for you.'

He passed over an envelope. Inside it was a bill of sale. 'I have received 5p from Martin Gurdon for the purchase of Honda Z600 OFV 215M.' My dad had bought a new car, his first, and had given me his old one. I was twenty and intensely excited.

My dad was driving a Citroën Visa E. This was a quirky-looking upright little five-door hatchback. Instead of stalks to work the indicators and wipers a pair of bean-can-shaped pods sprouted from either side of the instrument panel. They contained switches and levers to make these and other things work, looked peculiar, but were actually very effective. The rest of the car seemed oddly characterless.

This was not something that could be said of its Honda predecessor. Tiny, egg-shaped and growing frilly at the peripheries with rust, it looked like the wrath of God and its 600cc air-cooled twin-cylinder engine sounded like a fart in a biscuit tin. I couldn't wait to start driving it.

The wages I was scraping at the Press Association, paid weekly in little brown envelopes that contained cash, including four of the then new £1 coins, really didn't cover the costs of taxing, insuring and running this tiny car, and the long gaps between journalistic work meant that this made little financial contribution, but I was willing to more or less starve to death to have the pleasure of the Honda's company.

The Heinkel bubble car remained unfinished in the garden of my dad's boat, which itself still wasn't properly habitable. Perhaps he did not relish the idea of my piloting a minute 1950s 174cc three-wheeler on busy London roads. The Z was a quicker and relatively solid prospect by comparison. It would buzz along at 70mph without undue mechanical thrashing about, but torture it into the eighties and it felt very fast indeed. All its ignition parts (spark plugs, plug leads, points, condenser) and battery were well beyond their sell-by dates, which meant getting it started could be stressful. Such devilry as fuel injection and automatic chokes were alien to the little Honda, with its carburettor and choke knob that had to be hauled out before the engine was first cranked into life.

'Whrrr-whrrr-cough! Yeurg! Yeurg! Yearg! Yunk! Yunk! Yunk! Oooooo-yurgle!' it would protest on cold mornings before chugging into sullen inactivity. If these sounds were interspersed with infrequent ignition noises I would juggle accelerator pedal and choke in the hope of persuading it to keep setting light to the Two Star petrol that was its usual tipple, until these detonations became less infrequent and began to make the engine go round and round. Succeed in getting it started, and the Honda would have a go at charging up its fizzing old battery by way of saying thank you for waking it up.

At this point it would be time to try to make the car itself go. The boomerang-shaped gear lever, hinged under the dashboard, needed to be dropped down into second gear then gently pushed up into first, with a muted clunk. Release the handbrake and clutch, squeeze the throttle and the Z would begin rolling forward, engine note rising, the car sounding like a wasp whose voice had broken.

With Mini-like front-wheel drive and rack-and-pinion steering the little car didn't handle badly, but the steering itself was rather dead. The car was short and had crudely simple beam axle and cart spring back suspension, like a Silver Cross pram, so the Z had what can only be described as a skittish bottom on poorly surfaced roads. This was not the reason why, after a couple of weeks, I managed to collect a Ford Transit as a bonnet ornament. Quite how this was achieved in first gear and with the handbrake engaged is something I'll leave to your imagination, but I was lucky, as the Transit was parked when I embedded the Z into the middle of its hefty steel rear wheel. My pride and joy had a bust headlamp and restyled wing, bumper and bonnet, but the van was entirely undamaged, and its owner, a hulking builder, decided to be amused rather than turn me into chopped liver.

Fortunately all the crumpled bits were bolted rather than welded on, which is why I found myself on a pig farm in Surrey hunched over a wrecked Z rotting in a field, removing only slightly less rusty but unbent bits with a set of tools loaned by my father.

It rained, and when I hunched over a front bumper, cursing a nut that appeared to have been welded on, I felt a cold, damp sensation in the builder's crack area of my trousers. This turned out to be the moist nose of the farm's German Shepherd dog, which had padded up and was entertaining itself by rummaging around in my pants. Since I was wearing them too there wasn't much space. I somehow managed to get a bumper, bonnet and front wing home on a mix of buses and trains, and after much wrestling and cursing substituted these for the car's damaged bits. The new items were lurid orange rather than the rest of the car's matt yellow, so in its reconstituted state the Z now looked like an angry dwarf wearing an orange nose.

This didn't bother me, but made this already battle-scarred vehicle look spectacularly scruffy, and when the local police weren't stopping black youths in Ford Cortinas they took quite an interest in my tiny Honda.

I was overtaking a moped, something that required quite a

lot of revving, when a policeman appeared from between two parked cars, stepped directly into my path and held up his hand. As the moped trickled slowly past this truncheon-wielding apparition I shuddered to a halt inches from the policeman's neatly pressed black trousers, and through the windscreen stared up their owner's nose.

'How fast do you think you were you travelling?'

'About 25 miles an hour.'

'It sounded a lot faster than that.'

'I was only in second gear, and I have a little engine. Honestly, this is not a quick car.'

'Looking at it,' said the policeman, in a tone of slightly horrified awe, 'I'm inclined to believe you.'

I was negotiating Hammersmith Broadway when a large Police Rover fell in behind me, and I knew what would happen next. Just shy of Hammersmith Bridge its siren wailed and the blue lights on its roof lit up like a disco. I stopped and began climbing out of the car, which seemed to alarm the Rover's uniformed occupants, who flung themselves from it, apparently fearing that I was about to run away leaving them with the dreadful-looking Honda.

They poked and prodded, turned on lights, yanked at seatbelts, and seemed mildly disappointed that such a tatty-looking vehicle wasn't providing them with rich pickings for a prosecution. One of them began half-heartedly stirring the glove box's contents, at one point cursing when an ancient boiled sweet stuck to a finger of his gloved hand.

'Got any drugs in the car?' he asked.

'Of course officer, I've a stash of aspirin hidden in the spare wheel,' I thought, but actually said 'No.'

Before they reluctantly let me go, one of them eyed the Honda with open distaste and said, 'You can't really be surprised we stopped you, can you Sir?'

Not long after that the car revenged itself on one of his

colleagues. My grandmother was becoming less mobile, and I was increasingly taking her to the shops, the doctor and the man who tweaked her feet. These little trips, or the journey to one of her sisters, who lived in a large house in a village near Guildford, had improved our sometimes spiky relations, because I was, at last, doing something for her. The last time she'd said, 'Oh my God, darling,' was at a junction when I'd forgotten to engage the handbrake, and we'd gently rolled into the back of a Datsun Sunny estate car filled with small children, who'd turned and given us wide-eyed stares as two sets of chrome bumpers clashed and the Datsun shuddered on its stiff springs.

Gran had a hospital appointment when the Honda decided that it didn't want to start and flattened its battery. In desperation, I went in search of someone to help give it a push, and spied a large luxuriantly moustached motorcycle policeman astride a big BMW. He was wearing heavy waterproof gear, boots and a white open-faced crash helmet.

'Are you busy?' I asked.

'Yes,' came the monotone reply. I explained the situation.

'Hmmmm,' said the policeman. 'You want me to push your car for you?'

'It's just round the corner.'

When he saw the Honda slumped against the kerb, his lip curled under the moustache.

'You don't seriously drive around in that do you?'

We pushed and pulled the little car into the road.

'Get in,' said the motorcycle policeman, who was clearly a macho type. 'I'll push.'

Up and down the road we trundled. The Honda's back window was shaped like an analogue television screen, and I watched his face almost pressed against the glass. As it became increasingly red and sweaty I heard the policeman's heavy boots going 'Clomp! Clomp! Clomp!'

'It . . . will . . . start,' wheezed the puce-faced motorcycle policeman.

Two attempts later, after we'd rattled silently to a halt, the exhausted policeman flopped against the side of the car, drew a gloved hand across his crash-hatted head and whispered.

'No . . . it . . . won't.'

My grandmother used some of her meagre pension to buy me a new battery and made another hospital appointment, which in due course I took her to.

She was careworn and over six decades older than I was, and that car became a conduit between us; something which, to some extent, ameliorated the limitations age was imposing on her, and a space in which I began to discover my grandmother as a person.

During the Great War her mother had run a convalescent home for injured servicemen. Gran eloped with an airman called John Gurdon, putting a ladder to the upstairs window for him to climb down, so that they could run away and get married in secret.

As we negotiated a police-car-free Hammersmith Broadway we passed the Clarendon Hotel Ballroom next to the station, looking tired and tatty, and by then a music venue called the Klub Foot, a sweaty place that played host to punk and New Wave bands like the UK Subs.

'That was where I got drunk for the first time,' said Gran. At the time she'd not been much older that I was and had become a military driver, piloting an open Studebaker containing senior army officers.

'One of them took me to lunch at the Clarendon,' she said. 'We had a bottle of wine. Well I'd never drunk anything before and was quite squiffy once we'd finished. There was no question of my not driving. The traffic was coming in all directions, there were cars, trams, horse-drawn carts. I just put the car into gear and drove in a straight line and they all got out of the way.'

My grandfather, John Everard Gurdon, finished the Great War with 28 kills to his name and a DFC ('This officer is a brilliant fighting pilot who on all occasions shows great determination with entire disregard of personal danger,' read his citation). He suffered pain from a damaged hip, had a drink problem, was a skilled linguist and had aspirations to be a novelist. He was a man both made and damaged by his wartime experiences. By the late 1920s he'd published two novels and had been bankrupted. He and Gran were parents of three young sons, surviving on the rackety career my grandfather pursued in journalism and as the author of sub-*Biggles* adventures for magazines like *Air Stories* and *The Modern Boy*.

Both came from comfortable Edwardian families with servants, and were ill-equipped for a life that saw them moving from one rented flat to the next, at one point living in an old railway carriage in a Gloucestershire field. The first time my grandmother cooked a chicken, she put it into the oven whole and un-gutted. None of this was ever actively discussed, nor was my grandfather's eventual departure to Italy with a girlfriend, or the fact that for reasons apparently knotted up with Catholicism, there had never been a divorce. Gran had moved into the Hammersmith house in 1947, alone and very short of money. What became her basement flat had been completely unfurnished except for a grandmother clock, which remained on the wall of her small sitting room.

These things came out by degrees, and with them the realisation that the apparently severe, serious old lady was rather more complicated than I'd imagined. Once, as we buzzed and rattled out of London along the A3, thin bony fingers began massaging my chin, as my grandmother started chuckling.

'What are you doing?' I mumbled.

'Smooth as a baby's arse,' she said. 'Never mind.'

We were slowly overhauling a police Range Rover. Its occupants' looks of goggle eyed surprise at this strange little car and its strange occupants live with me still.

'What a funny car,' said my mother.

It was a warmer greeting than I'd expected. The cottage had a look of shabby organic neglect, and seemed to be sinking into a garden that had become wild. I'd parked in a spot where the Bristol 401 had once stood. It and BMW 700 were long gone, sold to people who had promised to restore them. Their absence seemed to represent a full stop to the childhood I'd left behind here a decade before.

'Would you like to go somewhere in it?' I asked. I'd grown to rather hate the village and the cottage. Going back had the quality of surviving an air crash only to keep returning to look at the wreckage as it rotted. I assumed my mother would feel the same. I was wrong.

'Who are you?'

'Martin.'

'I don't think so. You're too tall and your head's the wrong shape.'

How do you argue with that? Make a joke? 'I can't help growing or the shape of my head, would you like a ride in my car anyway?'

My mother was speaking again. 'If I go out, they'll break in to the house and steal. That's why you're here. I'm not having you steal from me too.'

She walked back to her tatty witch's cottage. 'And don't think you're coming in.'

The person she'd been would sometimes flicker to the surface, then slip beneath layers of anxiety that overrode everything else. Illness had burned through her like an acid, leaving her changed, and on days like this she was beyond reach. It hurt of course, but it wasn't personal. Her sisters and friends had all been given similar dismissals. Another visit on another day would reveal a different person, who could be welcoming, needy, or both.

'I'll come back later.'

'Don't bother.'

With me as its owner, the Honda became very scrofulous indeed. Its dunking in river water when my dad had bought it in 1979 meant galloping rot four years later. I patched, bodged and kept it going. Then the car became properly sick. It developed a persistent metallic clatter that indicated terminal bearing problems. Its big ends were on the way out, which for a car is every bit as painful as it sounds.

'You'll have to get another engine, or it's curtains,' said my dad.

I'd grown very fond of this strange little car and was unwilling to give up on it. We were a team, in a peculiar, human-inanimate object sort of way. Where could I find another engine?

'That scruffy heap of shit that you drive,' said Ken. 'There's one just like it at the garage over the road, but somebody's rammed it up the arse so it's even shorter than yours.'

This truncated little car ran sweetly. 'Give us fifty quid and you can take it away,' said the garage man. It meant living on £4 for a week and cycling to work in Fleet Street from Hammersmith in between paydays, but this seemed like a good investment.

I put the cars side by side, found that they came to bits with the relentless logic of a Meccano kit, and since they were front-wheel drive and all the mechanical bits sat on subframes which could be unbolted, three grown men could pick up their little bodies like giant wheel barrows, lift them over their engines, and swap them round, so with my dad and Ken's help, that's what I did. It took a weekend, but at the end of it I was driving a re-engined, clatter-free Honda.

'I didn't think you could do that,' said my dad. 'I'm impressed.'

Some of that driving left quite a lot to be desired, as I tended to handle the car's controls with the sensitivity of a bulldozer driver, and had one or two hair-raising lapses of concentration. The worst involved coming over the brow of a hill rather too quickly, to be confronted by a line of stationary cars about 150 yards ahead at some road works. It had rained and the road surface glistened. Despite knowing that I should pump the brake pedal to prevent the wheels locking, I panicked and glued my foot to it. During the massive skid that followed we fishtailed towards the traffic jam. I hung on to the steering wheel and waited for the impact. Instead we slithered to a halt with about ten yards to spare.

I once terrified a hitch-hiker on a motorway when, in a thunderstorm so severe that the wipers were struggling to clear water from the windscreen, we hit a patch of standing water which got between the Honda's tyres and the tarmac, and it shot sideways like a giant pond skater. We didn't hit the truck ahead of us, the tyres bit through the water and we carried on, more or less in a straight line, but the hitch-hiker, who until that point hadn't stopped talking, suddenly became very quiet.

Some first-time drivers kill the thing they love in weeks. I'd nearly succeeded with the Transit van incident, but in the end it took 18 months for me to finish it off, and I killed it with kindness.

It needed some structural welding, and I'd discovered a wild-haired collector of 1960s Honda S800 baby sports cars who said he would do this. He set fire to the car, not terminally, but enough to reduce its wiring loom to a smouldering mass.

'Ooo, sorry about that,' he said vaguely.

He promised to put things right with another wiring loom from a dead Z, but spent weeks not doing so. When eventually he got round to ineptly ramming the replacement loom into the Honda it worked for about a week, but then stopped charging its battery, and we were never able to find out why.

By then I was about to start my new job as a motoring PR man, which would involve a daily 70-mile commute. The poor old Honda had to go, and it was bought by a man who wanted the engine to power a strange little 1950s sports car called the Berkeley T60, which had one wheel at the back and was normally powered by a sputtering two-stroke British Anzani motorcycle engine. As I watched the moribund Z600 winched onto a flatbed lorry and driven away to its doom, I wasn't entirely surprised to find that there was a distinct lump in my throat.

# Mad Max

'Wazzock!'

We were being flung up the M4 motorway, travelling at about 100mph and closing fast on a gold Ford Granada. It was drifting past some trucks and coaches that were occupying the middle lane, travelling at about 20mph slower than we were.

'Why don't you get out of the fucking way, fuck knuckle?' said my boss.

A balding bull-necked South African in his mid-thirties, this man was an ex-motorcycle journalist known as Max, a name often prefaced with 'Mad', which he didn't mind at all. He'd been an anti-Apartheid activist and had come to Britain when draft papers for the South African army had arrived. He had lived in an East London squat, where my schoolfriend David had ended up. Max had given me a junior copywriting job at the Berkshire public relations firm where he worked on the basis of a sparse collection of cuttings, and the fact that one of my cousins was forging a journalistic career and knew Max's girlfriend, another journalist. Perhaps they reckoned that I would possess similar skills. If so, they were wrong.

On the surface Max was a noisy, harmonica-playing alpha male who said exactly what he thought, but this bigger/faster/funnier-than-you exterior concealed a thoughtful, cultured and academically gifted man with a world view that might have been described as 'romantic socialist'. Max was also a great deal kinder and certainly more complex than he appeared.

These layers did not extend to his driving, which was brutally quick, and so had the quality of pressing the fast forward button on the outside world. Thus the gold Granada was harried then dispatched.

This being the mid 1980s, Max had an expense account and a company car, although his approach to life was more Ernest Hemingway than Gordon Gecko. The car was a Toyota Corolla coupé, which sounds about as exciting as a Mother's Pride and margarine sandwich, but for those who know about such things it was a Corolla AE86, which had a fuel-injected twin-cam 1,600cc engine driving the rear wheels, and was designed to have the nuts revved off it without going bang. This slightly anonymous-looking car was light, impregnably built and went like stink, as Max was happy to demonstrate on high-speed commutes between Brentford and Reading.

The first journey was utterly terrifying. Max could drive well, but the way he drove wasn't gentle. Ham-hock hands would wrap themselves round the gear lever and steering wheel. These were slammed and jerked. Big feet applied crunching forces to brake, clutch and accelerator. The car roared, screamed, twitched and shuddered. Then it would be hurled through corners with horizon tilting, tyre sidewall-tugging force. The Corolla's engine's harsh mechanical din was usually competing with Capital Radio, thudding out the drum-heavy plastic pop that characterized the mid 1980s.

'AAAAAAAAAAAAAAAAAAAAAAAAAGGGGGGGGG-HHHHHHHHHHHHH!'

'WE BUILT THIS CITY ON ROCK AN ROLL!'

'AAAAAAAAAAAAAAAAAAAAAAAAAGGGGGGGGG-HHHHHHHHHHHHH!'

As musical turgidity combined with pure terror, I soon discovered hitherto unplumbed depths of physical coward-ice, clutching at the top of the hard plastic dashboard as I was pressed into my seat or shoved sideways by the G-force. Max clearly found my silent bug-eyed fear hilarious.

Having flung the Corolla from the motorway, he would then gleefully attack the A4 between Maidenhead and Sonning, filling the rear-view mirrors of unassuming Austin Allegro and Morris Marina drivers before flicking the Toyota to the right and squeezing past them as I silently prayed. Why we were never stopped by the police I don't know, but in a world without speed cameras, Max mostly got away with playing automotive Russian roulette, although a driving licence spattered with speeding points, which was perilously close to being revoked, indicated that 'the pigs,' as he called the police, had felt his collar more than once when I wasn't around. As the weeks progressed and we didn't die, I became inured to this panorama of speeded-up scenery and vehicular violence, and grew used to Max's verbal outbursts.

'Wake up, fuck knuckle!'

'Fuckwit!'

'What the fuck are you doing, wazzock?!'

The rage, although transient, was real, and I wonder now if it had something to do with the frustration of a really talented writer slumming it churning out literary bromides about car tyres and sponsored rally drivers who generally didn't win their rallies, and finding that the money, perks and easy professional life left a gap that became a well of frustration. This might be cobblers, but I suspect it was part of the occasional recklessness which seemed to drive this man.

Max's own car was a Rover P6 3500. This compact square-rigged saloon had a rumbling V8 engine. He referred to the Rover as 'Philby the monarch killer' for two reasons. Firstly, the car's body first appeared with a 2.0 litre four-cylinder engine as the Rover 2000 in 1963, the year Soviet spy Kim Philby was unmasked and fled to the Soviet Union. Secondly, a Rover 3500 was the car in which Princess Grace of Monaco was driving when she suffered a fatal crash in 1982.

By then my mode of transport was a Citroën Dyane 4, which

meant it was a re-bodied 2CV, with the same puttering 'flat twin' air-cooled engine, fifteen-inch wheels on skinny tyres, hammock seats, umbrella gear lever, soft ride and bonkers quantities of body roll on corners. It had the contours of a top hat made from origami paper. Most Citroën 2CVs used 602cc engines, but the Dyane 4 got by with 435ccs, so acceleration was distinctly glacial and hills were not its forte. It needed winding up and, on motorways, was little faster than the trucks and coaches with which it shared the inside and middle lanes.

I'd bought the car from my friend Jamie.

'The front brakes have a hydraulic leak, it needs the slave cylinder seals replaced,' he said.  ·

This meant taking off the front of the car, a simple job as the pressed tin bodywork was light and attached with a few nuts and screws.

The Dyane had drum front brakes, with all the braking gubbins concealed inside them. It also had an old-fashioned separate chassis frame with the engine, gearbox and drums sitting inside it. Officially, to detach the drums you first had to remove the driveshafts, because the chassis members got in the way of the drums being pulled clear. This was a big job, which Jamie decided could be circumnavigated. The car had incredibly long travel suspension, and could be bounced up and down like a nodding dog. One of Jamie's friends and I each put a foot on the front bumper and began to jerk the car up and down. On a particularly violent downward bounce Jamie wrenched a brake drum sideways along its driveshaft and over the chassis rail, risking mashed fingers or a smashed drum if he mistimed things and the drum slammed against the chassis. Miraculously it didn't, we effected repairs, bounced the drums back into position, and bolted the car back together. Soon afterwards I bought it.

The Dyane wasn't the ideal vehicle for twice daily rush hour motorway commutes, although I found that an extra 5mph or so could be gained by slipstreaming trucks. This basic little car contrasted rather with the 2.8 litre Ford Capri with a Janspeed turbocharger, owned by one of the PR firm's directors, and the brand new Rover 3500 Vitesse belonging to its boss. Occasionally he would appear in a beautiful 1920s boat-tail bodied Alvis 12/50 bought when he was a student.

Tall, raffish and some way into his fifties, this man appeared effortlessly elegant. He was a cross between Rex Harrison circa *My Fair Lady*, and Patrick Cargill, a suave comic actor who was a familiar face on 1960s and 1970s British television. He made an interesting contrast with Max.

Our employers were a civilised bunch. There was an art department where people did creative things, and account directors who were mostly men in their thirties, including one who bounced around like a puppy, but seemed to know personally anyone who died in motor sport accidents, and liked to wear a sombre face as he read their obituaries.

'Oh dear,' Max would say, 'so you've killed another one.'

How exciting could things get? I had my own desk with a typewriter and a phone, which was very modern and acted as a mini switchboard, with a row of red lights that glowed in a high-tech manner. The money was also a great deal better than anything I'd experienced before. I shared an office with Max and a copper-haired secretary who was chronologically a year or so younger than I was, but in every other way vastly more grown up. She was also married, pregnant and less than partial to me. I was allegedly in charge of her, but in reality the reverse was true.

For an ex-cycle messenger/bin bag salesman/photo deliveryman I was a brilliant copywriter (or 'PR executive' as my business cards laughably had it), but in reality I was pretty hopeless. I had little tact and no dress sense, and any latent ability I had as a writer was frequently subverted by an unusual approach to punctuation and spelling. Max, a skilled subeditor who'd earned good money freelancing on titles like *The Times*, had his work cut out policing my Tipp-Ex-spattered, error-laden efforts. This was still a word processor-free zone, so some pretty awful things escaped on to the paper.

One of my headlines about a rally driver caused Max to choke on a garibaldi biscuit.

'What is this?' he spluttered.

I blushed. 'Dougie In The Woods.'

'Nope. You've written "Dougie In The Weeds".'

I mostly churned out local newspaper press releases about rally and circuit racers sponsored by oil and tyre companies, and after every race I had to ring them up for quotes on their victories, or more often near victories.

One was a hulking circuit racer from Llanelli in Wales. He was a man of few words and I always found speaking to him unnerving.

'Hello,' I stuttered, 'how's the weather in Lan-nellie?'

Max had another chocking fit.

'LAN-NELLIE!' he chortled. 'You do realise that bloke's a Welsh nationalist? He'll be up the M4 to set light to your tower block before you can say "leek".'

As one cock-up collided with the next, panic filled the parts of my brain that should have been putting things right, so although I gradually improved, simply through churning out a lot of words, I kept getting things wrong.

We had to fill in time sheets documenting the work we'd done, and Max, half-jokingly, referred to mine as 'works of major fiction.'

Fortunately there would be a break, in the form of a camping holiday to north Wales with my friend David and his girlfriend Helen. David rode motorcycles, and at the time was piloting a Honda 400/4, which was a compact, elegantly engineered thing. Helen had been riding pillion when they'd been clipped by a car, resulting in her injuring her heel. She was on crutches and had to bathe the foot regularly, which was to prove interesting when camping.

'We'll put the tents in the car. I'll ride up, and Helen can travel with you,' David said.

The 250-mile trip was pretty exhausting, partly because I'd begun driving the little Citroën harder and harder, discovering that it could be pushed round corners at unfeasible speeds and unfeasible angles without actually falling over. Its cabin was so narrow that on right-hand bends I could brace my left foot below the passenger doorframe, wrench the steering wheel and scuttle round corners without actually sliding down the seat. This was fun at first, but ultimately reckless, and of course driving everywhere flat out was knackering for both the car and its occupants. Helen and I ended up with a form of 2CV tinnitus.

We camped in lush countryside near Porthmadog, sharing a field with some squaddies, who pinched our butter, and a collection of Harley-riding bikers from Bradford in Yorkshire. There were three strutting blokes in their twenties and a man old enough to be their father, who looked like a hard Bill Bailey, an image compromised somewhat by a pair of half glasses he used when tightening up the Allen bolts that constantly seemed to be vibrating loose on his throbbing, chrome-plated steed.

They all worked in the textile industry, and this was their annual break from repetitive, insecure jobs.

'Didn't think I was going to make this holiday,' said one. 'I was on the moors when a bloody sheep ran in front of bike and I hit it. That killed it, but the bloody thing had me off and I scraped half me fookin' arse up the road. Christ it hurt, so I took off me belt and leathered sheep. I wasn't hurting it, 'cos it was dead already, but I bloody felt better.'

He then yanked at the back of his trousers to reveal a portion of scarred arse.

The pubs weren't always welcoming to bikers and the locals weren't always keen on tourists. David was playing a slot machine in a pub when a short, round, smiley, middle-aged man approached him.

'See that chair over there?' he said, by way of opening conversational gambit. 'I'd like to break it over your head.'

'No mate, you wouldn't,' said David, giving the man one of his special looks.

The man thought for a moment. 'Actually,' he said, 'you're right.'

During the course of our stay we kept running in to a chubby bloke with bottle glasses, splayed teeth and frizzy hair. He appeared at the pubs we visited, on the streets outside them, and once at a flea market miles from where we were camping. He always greeted me with special effusiveness, suggesting that 'we must meet up for a drink.'

'He's friendly,' I said, a comment that reduced David and Helen to a state of hysteria.

'Friendly? Of course he's friendly. He's gay and he's trying to pick you up, you Muppet!'

Not being gay, but being very green, I hadn't realised. At the time I was highly alarmed at the discovery, viewing this lumpy opportunist as a terrifying gay stalker, when perhaps I should have been vaguely flattered, although thanks to the teeth, only very vaguely. I wonder now if similar opportunities with women had whistled by without my noticing them either.

Plenty of pubs had 'No Bikers' signs, and as we'd bonded with the Yorkshire bikers we'd get round this by parking up the road from our chosen boozer, they would fill my little Citroën with their crash helmets and leathers, then we'd make our grimy, but motorcycle-free entrance, to be served with icy politeness by the bar staff.

Drink made them mellow, familiarity made them fun. Under

the rather intimidating exteriors were streetwise innocents, socially awkward outsiders. We had a lot in common.

That holiday comes back to me now as a jumble of memories. Eating a dreadful Chinese meal and watching a Ford Granada estate trundle past the restaurant, its tailgate resting lightly on a coffin that was hanging out of the back of the car. We visited Britain's highest petrol station – don't ask – and afterwards, careering back to the campsite in the Citroën, I misjudged a corner, which suddenly tightened, and ended up on the wrong side of the road.

Ahead was a T-junction on which a petrol tanker was turning slowly but inexorably into our path. We were nose to nose by the time the Dyane shuddered to a halt and everyone had stopped screaming.

I returned to work with a trapped eyelid nerve so that I half-winked at people, and a streaming head cold.

The papers were filled with mostly uncomplimentary stories about the Greenham Common peace camp women, and the enthusiasm with which the police had prevented vaguely hippyish New Age travellers from reaching Stonehenge by smashing up the elderly coaches they'd turned into mobile homes.

'War on the Smellies!' screamed a gleeful *Daily Star*.

US President Ronald Reagan bombed Libya, in Russia the Chernobyl nuclear plant exploded, and when radioactive particles reached Britain we sat in the office wondering what exactly we were breathing in.

By then I was no longer staying with my grandmother. After 40 years living in the genteel chaos of her tatty Hammersmith townhouse, she had moved into a tropically hot sheltered flat. The raging Polish tenants departed without a murmur, my dad divided his time between his still half-finished houseboat and a long-term lady friend, whom I'd become aware of in my mid teens. A secondary school deputy headmistress, she values her privacy, so for the purpose of this narrative will remain semi-anonymous. Her approach to me was pragmatic. She gave my dad and me plenty of space, but stood no nonsense, and never attempted a parental role. Sometimes spiky, often funny, I never viewed her as a threat. She has become a very good friend.

Emptying the Hammersmith house of decades and skip loads of clutter was oddly moving. It felt like a death, and death itself wasn't far behind. My great aunt Joan, she of the foul mouth, fags and unfinished novel, grew quiet, shrank and withered away in a hospice, and once in her nice, clinical little flat with its red emergency cords, bathroom handgrips and an often absent warden, my grandmother began ailing too.

By then I'd moved into a first-floor bedsit in Chiswick, with a sink and an ancient, filthy Belling cooker. There was a communal toilet and a shower across the corridor. This either froze or boiled you, and in the winter a broken vent pumped freezing air into your face as the shower dribbled malevolently. Upstairs a young couple engaged in very loud domestics, which involved her hitting him, and once throwing him down the stairs.

They lived directly above me, and one night there was a terrific bang, as if a head had connected with the floor, and my bedsit door sprang open. I was busting for a piss but, half expecting to see a slight male figure flailing down the staircase and landing in a heap outside my door, I stayed put until the screaming abuse subsided and my bladder felt like a barrage balloon.

Ken, my dad's houseboat-dwelling friend, had been given a council flat twenty-one floors up in a block overlooking the M4 motorway in Brentford. Unwilling to part with his boat for another year or so, Ken offered to let me stay in the flat. 'Just pay me the council rent,' he said. So although this arrangement was illegal, he wasn't profiting directly from it.

The views of urban sprawl rolling to the horizon were

spectacular, particularly at night, the flat was vastly more homely than the grotty little bedsit, and free of its violent soundtrack, but also hermetically sealed and isolating.

My 'work/life' balance at this point had been knocked from its gimbal. I flailed from a job that was still on top of me rather than the other way round, to spending increasing amounts of time looking after my grandmother. Along with my father and cousins, I shopped, cooked, cleaned and generally did my best to prop her up and deal with the privations and indignities of extreme old age. She'd looked after me, and now it was my turn. This brought us closer together than either of us could have imagined. We'd gone from mutual dislike to mutual love. I felt an inadequate recipient of her emotional and physical dependence, but even then knew that to be on the receiving end of it was a privilege, and felt that if I never did anything else that was useful with my life, at least I'd done this.

That privilege came at a cost of stress that spread through the fibres of my body like ink infiltrating blotting paper, disrupting sleep, tightening every sinew and tendon and causing my heart to race.

And then my grandmother died, as we all knew she would. After yet another admission to hospital she'd taken control of her life for the last time and refused medication. She was her own person again, and no longer reliant on us.

'She asked how long it would take to die,' said a nurse. 'I said I didn't know. She was quite something, wasn't she?'

A day or so before, Gran had been propped up in bed, apparently asleep. Conversation between her visitors had all but dried up when she stirred, reached across, took my hand and brushed her lips against it. She wasn't the only one beyond speech at that point.

The effects of bereavement move at their own pace, leeching to the surface of a person's being until they are ready to give them back their lives, altered, but ongoing, and they can make their presence felt physically as well as emotionally. They made me rigid with tension, increasing a natural aptitude to knock over and break things. At work those things tended to be telephones. I swept them from desks, or trod on wires so that they were hurled to the floor. The agency's receptionist used a modular plastic switchboard with a wire that dangled over the side of her desk. I walked on this twice, the wire became taut, yanked the switchboard from the desk and its handset from the reception-ist's fingers, mid-call. As it hit the floor the switchboard's plastic clipped-together casing unclipped with a shattering bang and little keypad buttons with numbers on them scattered across the carpet. Unlike Humpty Dumpty, we were able to put it back together again afterwards.

Max and the secretary were elsewhere when I somehow poured tea into my desk phone. All its lights shone, and as I held it over a waste paper bin and brown liquid dribbled from it, nobody else could dial in or out. When a telephone engi-neer arrived and pronounced himself baffled I kept very quiet, and after a couple of hours of clandestine over-bin shaking, my phone's lights went out and the switchboard worked again.

Soon afterwards Max announced that he wouldn't be working for the agency. After a prolonged spat with one of the directors, he'd been made redundant. It took another six months of inglorious press release writing before the axe fell again, and I was, finally, its recipient. There had been a divorce amongst the directors, and I'd been one of its casualties. I'd felt a little numb but also quite relieved. This wasn't the right job for me, but I hadn't the self-confidence to walk away from it. Now

I needed to earn a living somehow, and began intermittent freelance writing again.

Since the money this raised was infrequent and notional, I also found a part-time job at a riverside pub in Richmond, where I discovered a lot more about the public than I'd ever learned in public relations.

# Viva Hate

When I asked why he was selling the Vauxhall Viva the plumber's response was simple.

'I hate it.'

By the time I sold that car, I hated it too. I loathed the way it looked, drove, even the way it smelled inside. It was far removed from the Bristol 401 I fantasised about owning.

That Vauxhall's single merit was that it kept me mobile. I'd bought it for £250 because the 1960s Rover 2000, which I'd foolishly purchased to replace the Citroën Dyane, was resting once too often, thanks to a clutch pedal that was refusing to work with the clutch despite the component that made this happen having been replaced for the third time. Then there was the £80 Fiat 127, a white three-door hatchback with nothing in the way of heating, a rusty door, and a driver's seat backrest that had collapsed. Its clutch worked better than the Rover's in that it at least worked, but had started to slip.

I'd stopped the seat collapsing by ramming a large offcut of tree, found in Richmond Park, between it and the rear passenger footwell, which could have done terminal things to my spine had anyone driven into the back of the car.

I could feel it through the seat, and when I came to sell the Fiat because the clutch was too expensive to fix, the piece of tree was still there. The person who eventually bought the car did so in high summer, and failed to test the non-functioning heater. Nor did he notice the Fiat's habit of jiggling up and down on smooth road surfaces, thanks to flat spots on its tyres.

However, he was shorter than me, so when it came to the test driving, he'd sat in the driver's seat and pulled it forward. I was sitting next to him and had no option but to reach behind his seat and adjust the piece of wood, more or less slamming it into his back as I did so. Miraculously, the seat stayed upright and he didn't notice my flailing about, or apparently being rammed in the back.

This man paid £110 for the dreadful vehicle, and said he lived in Uxbridge. Would I mind following him back in his old car whilst he drove the cursed Fiat?

It was a long journey, during which I expected the Fiat's seat to fail, but amazingly it didn't. The tension continued for another half an hour after we'd parted and I waited for a bus to take me home, half expecting the purchaser to storm into view demanding his money back.

Selling a car in that state was a mean trick, even though I was broke. I don't believe in Fate, but if I did, than I'd have said owning the Vauxhall Viva was its way of making me pay for it.

It was an 'HC Viva,' circa 1975, which meant it was the third generation of this car. Launched five years earlier, it had a strong-but-agricultural engine, a strip speedo and an interior with the aesthetic of a pedestrian subway in Thamesmead. The estate car body was almost good-looking, more of a low-slung hunchback hatchback than a box on wheels, but the car's looks were undermined by those wheels, which were inset, rather like sofa castors. Mine was painted a faded matt yellow on the outside, with a spray tagged hieroglyphic adorning one of the side windows. I seem to remember Steve Coogan's character Alan Partridge had something similar on the side of his Rover 800. Inside the Viva's décor was an unappetising mix of scratched painted metal, vinyl seats and grainy hard plastic. The last two were the sort of brown colour you might find inside the nappy of a very small, very ill baby.

The doors closed with a tinny clang, but the tailgate virtually refused to shut if you were foolish enough to unlatch it, something that necessitated poking a finger or screwdriver into the hole where the lock button had once been and pushing a little metal foot that sat behind it. Inside was a constant swirl of plaster dust, because the plumber had used the Viva as his van, and every crevice of its stark interior was filled with the stuff. On summer afternoons you could see dust cascading like fairy dandruff in the sunlight. Then there were the old washers and offcuts of copper pipe. I made several attempts at cleaning its interior, but every so often a new plumbing remnant would appear on its threadbare carpet.

Driving it was a lowering experience, because the seating position meant that you more or less sat on the floor, with your nose almost level with the top of the steering wheel, peering at a featureless rectangle of yellow bonnet.

There was a deadness about the Viva's controls. This infected everything from the floppy stalk that made the indicators slowly flash and the windscreen wipers, with their brittle rubber blades I was too poor to replace, scrape across my line of vision, to the precise-but-clonking four-speed gearbox, whose internal components were not to be rushed.

The steering had an inert, rubbery weightiness and could barely be bothered to self centre, so the car had to be steered like a motor cruiser in a swell, with a great deal of wheel twirling. Conversely, when negotiating sharp bends or roundabouts, the steering always seemed to need more lock than its driver was expecting, and this meant last minute wheel jerkings with the result that the Viva felt as if it was being steered round a giant 50 pence piece. It rode with a weird combination of compressive squishiness and bone-shaking harshness, unless it was laden with gear.

A full load never had much impact on its performance, since its 1256cc engine always felt as if someone had fitted a concrete mixer's flywheel to it. As for the way the engine breathed, you could almost hear it sucking in air, like a swimmer who'd swallowed a waterlogged corn plaster and was trying not to choke.

By now London's roads were teeming with thrusting corporate types driving Volkswagen Golf and Peugeot 205 GTIs, cutting a swathe through or cutting up the diminishing ranks of 1960s and 1970s tin boxes like my Viva. The Golfs and Peugeots had a mix of style, competence and a sensible aspiration. Now they have a nostalgia value for many of the people who owned them, because they were fun.

The 1980s has a reputation for selfish vacuity which to some extent it deserved. A lot of people did have a good time during the decade, but for those who found the era's surface gloss unattractive, watching them grew a bit galling, especially if, like me, you worked in a London riverside pub which every weekend was packed with such people. I wasn't jealous of their lifestyles, which often seemed to depend on owning stuff, and appeared to have an elemental competitiveness and a pecking order that revolved round clothes, white goods, houses, holidays and pay packets.

Some did conform to the braying, finger-snapping giant-cellular-phone-and-Porsche-key-ring-on-the-bar cliché of the age, and they clearly felt that arrogance was a badge of honour, but this often had an insecure tinge and was easy to prick with a sharp word or a look of contempt.

I do remember one packed Sunday summer lunch when every seat in the pub was taken. I'd arrived late thanks to the Viva having one of its refusing-to-start mornings. When I finally got to work, feeling harassed and with oil and muck wedged under my fingernails from yanking at filthy, over-the-hill spark-plug leads, I was greeted frostily by the landlady, a solid, not-to-be-messed-with matriarch who'd once chased a regular customer for a mile along the towpath, hair streaming and kitchen apron flapping as she shouted oath-laden threats after he'd jestingly called her 'the Witch of Endor.'

Not wishing to blot my copybook further I'd got on with cleaning the pub's brassware, including the urinal's 'sparge' pipe and the toilets themselves. Oddly enough, this wasn't my favourite job, but after feeling a bit off-colour a week after I'd started doing this regularly, my immune system had become supercharged and I'd been ailment-free for months.

Bog cleaning out of the way, I helped stack up the bar with washed glasses and new drinks bottles, and when the pub opened I was soon hard at work, collecting glasses and delivering food. I'd ignored one group of drinkers who'd tried attracting my attention by pointing at me and snapping their fingers, and tuned out the wailing of some particularly obnoxious children and their parents' ineffectual attempts at placating them.

'Jocasta darling.'

'No, Mummy.'

'Jocasta . . . Jocasta, leave Jonty . . . '

'Don't 'noy me. Don't 'noy me.'

'Jonty doesn't like that Jocasta. JOCASTA! Oh Jocasta! Now you've poked him in the other eye.'

Despite stuff like this I actually enjoyed the work. It forced me into the company of other people, and I'd begun to appreciate the camaraderie of my working environment. This was a shared experience, and my colleagues were an interesting mix of ages and backgrounds, either passing through on their way to better things, or just earning a living.

One of them was a tall, elegant girl, serving food as a means of repaying her massive student overdraft of about £600. I'd come to the conclusion that I rather fancied her, although I was given no encouragement.

The pub garden was reached by walking down a flight of stone steps, and people who'd ordered food were given numbered tickets. One of my jobs was to deliver the food, calling out the numbers at the top of the steps.

The Girl I Fancied handed me a tray with four cottage pies in oval earthenware dishes. I made for the top of the steps and called out the number. The garden was teeming with drinkers. Spotting the pie people I made for them, lost my footing and started tap dancing down the stairs. As the tray clanged to the ground, I began juggling hot cottage pie pots. Two hit the deck and shattered, but I somehow grabbed the other pair, finding that I'd clutched them to my chest,

I was wearing an elderly purple sweatshirt which, once I'd removed the pies, now had two oval potato rings at tit level. Instead of having nice white fluffy tops the pies were now grey and lightly coated with a fluff of man-made purple fibres. In the deafening silence that followed a cultured voice said, 'I don't think we'll have those, if you don't mind.'

The Girl I Fancied seemed highly amused by this. Crimson with embarrassment, I left the shirt-enhanced pies by the serving hatch and went to clean up. When I returned, spud ovals replaced by less obvious grease marks, the pies had gone, and the Girl I Fancied was red in the face and close to tears. What could be the matter?

'A very pushy woman came up and insisted on being served at once,' she said. 'Then she saw "your" pies and said "I want those. I don't want any of the others. It's those or nothing," so I didn't argue.'

I asked if this woman had been rude and upset her

'I'm not upset, but I am about to have hysterics. She's out there now, eating your shirt.'

My existence was still pretty hand to mouth. I tended to cut corners to save what cash I had, and that included car

maintenance, which meant the Viva's ancient sparkplugs, points, distributor cap, plug leads and battery were forced to keep working long after they should have retired. At the pub I'd taken to parking the car on a road that was on a slope, then turned sharp right. Beyond it was the river, separated from the road by some railings. When there was no other traffic I'd open the Viva's driver's door, pull out the choke, switch on the ignition, release the handbrake, push the car and as it gathered speed I would jump in, bang it into second gear and let out the clutch, which usually bump-started the engine into life and saved the battery some work. Why we never crashed through the railings and into the river I don't know.

By now the old battery was getting very sick. Just how sick I discovered when travelling over Kew Bridge on a wet night. The rain had forced me to use the lights, windscreen wipers and demister fan. Every time the car stopped, the lights dimmed like depressed glow worms and the fan slowed, so I'd rev the engine, the alternator would pump out more juice which brightened the lights and sped up the fan, giving the battery some respite. But its condition was terminal and that night the battery had had enough. I'd crested the bridge and was coming down the other side when there was a terrific 'bang!' All the lights went out and the engine died. I had quite a lot of momentum so was able to coast down the road, exit the bridge, and by a miracle trundle into a parking bay. I climbed out of the moribund car, opened the bonnet and by the light of a street lamp was surprised to see that the engine bay was wet and the battery had disappeared. Then I saw the shards of black plastic and realised that it had committed suicide, exploded and spattered everything with acid. I found some old newspaper and did my best to mop up the acid so that is wouldn't strip the paint from the Viva's engine bay. Then, fingers tingling and burning slightly from the acid that was now on them too, I trudged sadly on. Twenty-four hours later, using the new battery I'd finally been forced to buy, I fired up the car, amazed at the speed its starter motor turned over when working properly. Although the paint under the bonnet was now a bit streaky, everything still seemed to function properly so I headed for home, but on the way quickly discovered that none of the lights, including the indicators, worked any more.

Finding that the car's fuses hadn't died, I began removing light bulbs and discovered that they'd all blown. When the battery had obliterated itself it had taken every single lamp with it. Replacing them was painfully expensive, but it had to be done, with the exception of the ones that illuminated the instruments. I simply couldn't get the binnacle that housed them out to change them. This meant that at night I wasn't able to tell how fast I was going or how much fuel I had left, and in the end took to carrying a torch, with which I would scan the instruments at intervals, or time looking at them when street lamps were in the right place to light them up. This was not, I felt, what being a putative motoring journalist should be about.

Then a friend expressed interest in buying the awful old Vauxhall. He bought it and kept it alive for another five years, never tiring of telling me how much he liked it.

I needed every penny I could get, and I needed a real job. My dad and I had been infected by all the 1980s 'property-owning democracy/right to buy' stuff. He'd decided to fund the purchase of a second houseboat, which resembled a floating shoebox and was moored just below Richmond Bridge.

'I'll put some savings into it, but you have to get a real job, and earn some money,' he'd said.

So every week I'd buy the *UK Press Gazette* and Monday's *Guardian*, which contained a media jobs supplement, and apply for every junior reporting position I saw. Writing about cars full time for a living seemed more remote than ever, and time was sliding by. I had quite a decent selection of cuttings and started to get interviews, although I wasn't getting jobs at the end of them. Then I answered an advertisement so vague that I wasn't sure that it was actually for a journalistic position. I was interviewed by two women. One, a senior personnel officer, grilled me relentlessly. The other said she was the editor of a trade magazine specialising in employment and industrial relations. It was a new launch and she was looking for a reporter. The questions were tough and I left feeling frazzled and depressed.

'I bet you'll get that job,' said my dad.

I told him ungraciously that I wouldn't. A week later a letter arrived proving him right.

# The Best Worst Car

'What is a Morris Marina?'

The question startled me, because the person asking it was Raul Pires, who'd styled the modern Bentley Continental GT.

In the interconnected world of car building, Bentley, whose extreme Englishness lies at the heart of its appeal to the Chinese, Russians, Americans and Indians who bankroll its cars, is actually owned by Volkswagen, a German firm, and Pires, a dapper, friendly man barely into his forties when I met him, is Brazilian.

But his question made me think. The Marina was also a quintessentially British car, but not in a good way. It was parochial and expedient, perhaps the ultimate example of why the old British car industry, the one that had flourished in the first half of the twentieth century, bit the dust well before the end of it. Basically, the people who made the Marina knew it was crap, but expected Britons to buy it out of patriotic duty. Oddly, a lot of them did.

From the 1970s to the mid 1990s Marinas were everywhere. Then they died out, probably about the time when Raul Pires was learning his trade. Why would he have seen one?

So his question was almost anthropological. This was a car designer's equivalent of a gynaecologist discussing a nearly extinct strain of thrush. And this man was asking me because I'd owned one of these cars. Yes, I'd been a Morris Marina carrier.

Perhaps this has rotted my brain, because even though I knew the Marina was dreadful, I grew very fond of mine, although I think that fondness was largely situational. The car's arrival coincided with and abetted a happy period of life, elements of which have endured ever since.

After the miserable privations of Vauxhall Viva ownership, I'd had a car-free period, and enjoyed it. When I felt wistful about cars it was usually at rain-lashed, late-night bus stops, or sharing railway carriages with people who were pissed, aggressive or mad, but mostly my head was filled with other things. Thanks to landing a proper job on a magazine, I was turning into a real journalist, rather than an amateur writer who couldn't earn a living from his words. Being a reporter on a fortnightly trade magazine called *Personnel Today* wasn't glamorous and it wasn't writing about cars, but my colleagues were motivated, talented and supportive, and I learned more in the first six months there than in the entire period since I'd left school. It was wonderful.

They wanted a junior reporter, someone who could track down sources, get quotes from them and identify news angles. I had no idea how to do this, and blundered about for the first couple of weeks terrified I'd screw up. Perhaps because the magazine was a new launch and they hadn't time to get anyone else, they persevered with me, and the news editor, a bear-like giant, nearly 6'8" tall, who despite being 27 and only four years older than me, liked to call me 'lad', quickly got what made me tick.

'You work best with a size fourteen boot six inches from your backside.'

He'd said this after I'd written a news story that was total gibberish.

'Do it again,' he said.

I had fifteen minutes before catching a train to London for a press conference and told him there wasn't time.

'In that case we'll just leave some white space and a caption saying, "Martin didn't have time to write a decent story here",' said my boss. I thought he meant it, probably because he thought so too.

Ten minutes later he finished looking at the thing I'd banged out and gave me a flinty smile.

'That,' he said, 'is the first decent piece of work you've done. Now you've five minutes to catch the train, so bugger off.'

I felt like a failed alchemist who'd finally got a spell right. After that I'd pursue stories like a dog worrying a bone, and keep going until, more often than not, I got the information we needed. Quite by accident, I'd found a job that suited the way my brain worked.

This was an era where British Airways ran a foul advertisement involving a bunch of boardroom slimeballs talking about screwing a colleague over a business deal because he'd be knackered after a long-haul flight, only to be confronted by a suited, exfoliated male model type who was daisy fresh and ready to screw them thanks to flying BA.

This man would have been driving a Porsche, which was very much a 1980s status symbol, rather than a Morris Marina, which was already a talisman for all that was wrong with the 1970s, but when one of my neighbours decided to emigrate and put his Marina up for sale, I began to feel covetous about the car, although as a motoring 'expert' I knew this was wrong.

Launched in 1971, the Marina was one of the first, and nastiest, spawn of British Leyland, a conglomeration of once independent carmakers including Rover and Jaguar, and what had been the British Motor Corporation, makers of Minis and Morris Minors. British Leyland was soon beset by internal rivalries, an often ageing selection of cars that competed against each other, calamitous industrial relations and dumb business decisions. Conceived in eighteen months as a rival to the all-conquering Ford Cortina, and as a replacement for the greatly loved Morris Minor, the Marina was lashed together using old bits of Triumphs, MGs, Morrises and Austins, and was, frankly, cobblers. It wasn't bad-looking, but it was an evil thing to drive. It 'understeered.' Understeer is a technical term that basically means that when confronted by a corner a car is reluctant to go round it, and instead tries to keep going in a straight line.

The Marina had either a 1,300cc A Series engine, which first appeared in the bubble-shaped 1951 Austin A30, or an 1,800 'B Series', found in the MGB and dating from 1953. Both were strong and crudely willing, but the heavy B Series was like a lump of pig iron when stuffed under the tinny Marina's bonnet, and the car struggled to haul this great weight round bends. The smaller-engined Marina was a bit better, but still had the dynamic poise of a drunk tripping over a paving slab. Despite their simplicity, early Marinas went wrong a lot. Gearboxes expired and things broke or dropped off, a process abetted by bored, fractious, strike-prone assembly line staff, who nailed them together without enthusiasm. In America one owner was said to have taken his Marina back to the dealer because it made a strange rolling/rumbling noise. After weeks of searching this was traced to the sill (a hollow area of the car's substructure below the doors), which was cut open to reveal a bottle. Inside the bottle was a note that read: 'So you've found it then.'

This sort of self-indulgent career death wish was in retreat by the late 1970s, even if British Leyland's industrial relations were at a strike-bound nadir and the company was fighting for survival. In the middle of this chaos BL gave the Marina a makeover, christening the end result the 'Marina 2,' in which form the car became only mildly unpleasant and pretty reliable. Dating from 1978, the one being sold by my neighbour was a Marina 2 1.3 'Special'. A fat-bottomed four-door saloon, it was painted a slightly faded wine red. It had reversing lights, a vinyl roof and comedy plastic wood on the dashboard. Its seats were covered in cloth rather than sticky vinyl, and it had a radio with a cassette player. Since the owner wanted £350 it was beyond my pocket, but a couple of weeks before he was due to leave the clutch began to play up.

'You can have it for £25,' he said.

The car had a long MOT and could still be driven in a juddering, jerky sort of way, so I bought it. The engine was weary and clattered when first started, then the internals would heat up, expand and fit together more snugly, at which point it sounded remarkably healthy. The car burned much of the oil that was supposed to lubricate its engine, which meant pouring more in at regular intervals, so I never did a proper oil change.

Up to 30mph it was surprisingly lively, but otherwise painfully slow, yet its engine had a charming indomitability and pulled this clumsy car along like a tractor. The heater worked, the seats were comfortable, and even had front headrests. I could play music on its cassette machine and the car gave me an immense sense of freedom. It was a lot better than no car at all.

The Marina's crudity made it very easy and inexpensive to fix, thanks to a plentiful supply of parts in scrapyards. It was also cheap to run and mostly reliable. The Marina might have been a woeful new car, but it was a great old banger. Who wouldn't be impressed with that? Not the Girl I Fancied.

'A Morris Marina,' she scoffed, 'for £25?'

Oh well. She'd deign to ride in it if we were the best things on offer, and the car didn't actually look that scruffy, at least to start with, until a GP's wife drove her husband's BMW into its side. She was at a road junction on a give way line. The Marina and I were grinding along a main road towards her. Briefly I thought I wanted to turn left by the BMW, signalled, realised I didn't, switched off the indicator and kept going for another six feet until this lady T-boned the side of my cheap old car with her husband's expensive one.

'He was signalling to turn left!' she screeched, over and over again, despite being told by a policeman, who'd turned up to see if anyone was hurt, that I'd had right of way, so it didn't really matter what I'd been doing with my indicators.

Inspecting the battered Morris I was quite cheered. The two

doors on the passenger side were scraped and buckled, and the front one refused to open, but these could be unbolted and replaced. The rest of the car looked straight and damage-free.

Several weeks later, after the insurers had looked at the car and said they thought it was beyond economic repair, I paid £12 for a couple of scrapyard doors and bolted them on. One was white, the other a faded grey, but both were un-dented and they opened and shut properly.

'It looks a bit like a very scruffy American police car,' mused the Girl I Fancied.

Shortly after that the doctor's wife's insurer phoned. 'Our client is mad,' he said. 'If we give you £200 for the car, will you go away?'

I said yes, but added that I wanted to keep the Marina.

'No problem,' said the insurer. 'We don't want it.'

So my £25 Morris ended up costing -£175, and I began to bond with it. Even the Girl I Fancied seemed to have softened to the car, and began referring to the old heap as 'Morris,' as if this was its Christian name.

Further bonding occurred when somebody tried to steal Morris by smashing the driver's window, pouring acid on the door, trashing the steering column combing, indicator and wiper stalks and then tearing the wiring from the ignition switch. After all this effort they failed to hot-wire it. Ten quid went on another white driver's door and I fixed the ignition wiring with a mix of block connectors and insulation tape. Using Blu-Tack I reattached the indicator stalk into the hole from which it had been ripped, but this stalk had also made the horn work, and was clearly beyond doing so now. But I had a brainwave. Not long before, a student had driven his VW Beetle into Morris's backside and smashed the car's single foglamp, so I wired the horn through the now redundant fog lamp switch on the dashboard. This was an on/off type switch, which meant I could sound the horn, steer and gesticulate all at the same time.

The 1980s were about to morph into the allegedly less carnivorous 1990s, but I still had cause to use my homemade
horn switch on the North Circular Road, somewhere north of
Finchley, on my way to the loveliness that was Ilford.

Morris and I were on our way to see the Girl I Fancied, who
had moved into an Ilford bedsit because she'd landed her first
teaching job in still-lovelier Romford. When the wind was
blowing the right way the place was within inhaling distance
of the Romford Brewery. I'd helped her move into the bedsit
the week before, and by way of thanks she'd offered to feed me
the following Saturday evening. I didn't go home until late on
Sunday afternoon, rattling round the North Circular, grinning
like an idiot. What had changed her mind about me? It wasn't
my career prospects, clothes sense or piebald Morris Marina.

I resolved not to find out, just in case I screwed up whatever
it was and she changed her mind back again. Somewhere near
Cockfosters I was cut up by a tatty Transit van. Instead of the
anger I normally felt, I smiled and waved.

The Girl I Fancied was called Jane, and Morris became an
important part of our lives, especially when we decided to spend
a weekend in Norfolk. We'd booked a B&B in Norwich, which
the Ramblers' Association claimed was within easy walking distance of the city centre. Our route then took us into the Essex
countryside, with its broad flat fields and villages with thatched
roofed cottages painted Battenberg cake pinks and yellows.
Roads like these, where nudging the speedometer above 50 was
an unusual event, suited Morris's tired, heaving suspension, but
the noise of the car's throbbing engine and its heavy inert steering made progress hard work. When we rattled into a market
town called Halstead, it felt as if we were far from home. We followed a strong smell of ageing cooking fat to a transport café and

bought restorative cups of tea. In fact, we'd gone less than fifty miles, and when, hours later, we finally wheezed into Norwich it was growing dark. Jane, Morris and I were all exhausted, but mildly elated. Our £25 car had survived a 114-mile journey without anything detaching itself or going wrong.

Our elation dipped when we saw the bed and breakfast. It consisted of two scruffy Edwardian houses painted blood red, with a gap between them that functioned as a car park, but presumably had once been filled by another house. It looked like a Second World War bombsite and probably was. The lobby was thick with dust. We were eyed by an ancient, cobwebbed security camera, a moth-eaten German Shepherd and a tiny, scowling old woman, who ran the place and exuded ill will.

'You can leave your car in the car park if you want, but if anybody steals it that's your lookout,' was her opening gambit. We said we thought this would be unlikely.

'Old banger, is it?' she said, looking me up and down in a way that implied that this was what she expected. I nodded.

'The fact it isn't worth anything doesn't mean it's safe,' she said with something approaching relish. 'They'll nick anything round here. Here's your room key.'

A large key was slapped on to the desk. We asked if there was anywhere to eat.

'Beefeater,' said our host, jerking a wizened thumb in the direction of the road we'd just travelled down. 'There's nothing else. Oh yes, you'll need to drive. It's too far to walk.'

Our room was in the other building, and reached by a sort of outdoor corridor running along the back of the car park. Roofed with corrugated iron, its sides were made of chainlink fence, and it would have looked perfectly at home in an open prison. The room itself had swirling patterned carpets and wallpaper that screamed '1973.'

'I think this bed's damp,' said Jane, pulling back the blankets and feeling the sheets.

Suddenly, the Beefeater seemed very enticing. We were the only customers, and made the mistake of asking the waitress what sort of day she'd had.

'Do you want to look at my burn?' she said, waving the back of her hand under our noses so we could see a dull red welt.

'I did that on a frying pan this morning. The manager shouted at me and made me cry . . . what would you like to drink?'

Later, the manager appeared and asked if we were enjoying our food, then proceeded to tell us that his wife had left him because she couldn't stand working in catering. 'It's very stressful,' he confided. 'I keep having issues with portion control. We're giving people too many peas.'

Giving people too much of anything wasn't an issue for the B&B matriarch as she served breakfast the following morning in what looked like a prefabricated 1950s classroom. It was filled with single mothers and rangy, grizzling small children.

'Bed and breakfast families,' said Jane, as Grandma appeared with our cooked breakfasts that consisted of cold toast, rubberised fried egg, congealed baked beans and thin, flinty slices of bacon.

Something made me rebel, and I said, 'Can I have a second piece of bacon?'

Without a word our hostess bustled back to the kitchen, slamming the door behind her, returning with a freezing side plate on which resided a second cremated offcut of pig. Banging this down in front of me she smiled nastily and hissed, 'There you go, Oliver Twist!'

We thoroughly enjoyed the sheer awfulness of this, and the rest of our weekend, which was far from awful, as we clattered into the otherworldly Norfolk countryside, with its dark brown earth and roads running above ruler straight culverts, along which Morris happily lolloped.

On subsequent weekends we would clamber into the car and head for the rolling Essex countryside, Morris lumbering gamely past ex-council houses, then a desolation row of villas often painted shocking pinks or lime greens, adorned with fibreglass Doric columns, and hidden behind gates and high walls topped with depressed-looking but rampant lions and griffins, before the countryside opened up and the gaudy houses petered out.

This was very much Margaret Thatcher's natural constituency, but as the weeks went by and the girl of my dreams didn't give me my boyfriend P45, it was starting to look as if Thatcher might not be so lucky. Those who'd really adored her and the rest who'd voted for her as the least worst option were falling out of love.

Having introduced a tax on every adult citizen for local services, called the 'Community Charge' by its backers but the 'Poll Tax' by everyone else, it looked as if Mrs Thatcher and her increasingly weary cohorts had finally bitten off more than they could chew.

Replacing a tax where only the people who owned houses paid for local public services also used by everyone else with something where they chipped in too wasn't unreasonable, but using Scotland as a test bed for it was typically punitive. Then the Poll Tax was introduced in one hit everywhere else.

As we rattled through the spring countryside, Morris's radio was alive with the Poll Tax riots in central London. There was a sense of national fury that looked likely to find its voice in the ballot box. After ten years in charge, Mrs Thatcher appeared ever more shrill and harsh, a living caricature of the way she was often viciously portrayed in newspaper cartoons, but she clearly had no plans to quit the driving seat. Jane, meanwhile, revealed her own driving aspirations as we pottered down a lane.

'Would you show me how to drive Morris?' she asked.

We found a dirt track that led to a tiny dark stone church with a squat steeple, surrounded by fields, and Jane climbed behind the wheel.

'What do those pedals do?' she asked, peering at the clutch, brake and accelerator.

I explained, telling her that she needed to get the engine spinning to stop the car stalling when moving off. Jane treated clutch and accelerator like a pair of on/off switches; in the case of the accelerator this meant mashing it into the carpet, then releasing the clutch with a bang. Kicking up dust and gravel, Morris began lurching and bunny-hopping towards some abandoned farm machinery, which appeared to have a row of rusty talons at the front. At this point I realised that Jane was using the steering wheel as something to hold on to rather than steer the car. As the talons rushed towards us I made a suggestion.

'Get your foot . . . Your FOOT! GET YOUR FOOT OFF THE ACCELERATOR!'

One of Jane's elegant leather boots was transferred from the accelerator and slammed down on the brake, but she hadn't disengaged the clutch, and I was so panic-stricken that I hadn't noticed. Fortunately Morris's normally lethargic brakes had enough inertia to make the engine labour and stall, and we juddered to a halt in a cloud of dust about ten feet away from the lethal farm implement. We stared at this for several seconds until Jane spoke.

'That was fun,' she said. 'Can we do it again?'

So we did. She learned quickly, and it wasn't long before Jane mastered the choreography of controls that made Morris steer, go and stop. Soon the car was adorned with a pair of L plates, and we spent much of our weekends trundling down Essex country lanes, getting in the way of angry-looking young men in white Ford Escort XR3is.

There were moments of excitement, notably the time when we lurched round the Gants Hill roundabout signalling right when we actually wanted to go left, but unable to do anything about this other than make frantic hand signals because the indicator stalk had fallen off and then vanished under the driver's seat. Yet the driving lessons seemed to cement our relationship rather than sink it, even if reversing round corners over and over again did make things a little tense. I'd never taught anyone to do anything before and it was a novel, not to say heartening experience to find that I could.

As 1990 dawned, in between reversing round corners and practising hill starts – not easy thanks to Morris having a very ropey handbrake – Jane and I talked about the way Poland, Hungry and Czechoslovakia had detached themselves from being client states of the Soviet Union, and watched as East and West Germans smashed down the Berlin Wall. Later I was driving Morris through a Christmas-time traffic jam in suburban Sutton, listening to the radio as potato-faced Romanian dictator Nicolae Ceauşescu and his gaunt wife Elena were toppled. I heard their world unravelling minute by minute during that journey. When the pair were shot by firing squad on Christmas Day, we concluded that for the average Romanian this was a very good present.

Eleven months later a less lethal political drama finally exploded in Britain, as the leonine-haired Michael Heseltine, who'd stalked from Mrs Thatcher's cabinet in a row over helicopters, finally challenged her for the leadership of the Conservative Party.

All the while the driving lessons continued, but we realised that Jane needed professional help to pass her test, so she enlisted the assistance of a driving instructor called Mervin. A short, squat character with a friendly reptilian face and a bottomless well of patience, he was chosen by Jane because he'd got a 60-something neighbour through her driving test at the twelfth attempt, and although otherwise very sweet, she was one of the most potentially lethal drivers imaginable. Mervin had at least been the one who'd facilitated getting her a licence to kill. If he could do that, then teaching Jane would be a breeze.

As the date of her driving test arrived, the wider world looked very different from the way it had when she'd first hurled Morris down that farm track.

On the day of her test, the rake-thin, bloodless examiner with a clipboard, who'd stiffened noticeably when he first saw the car, clambered into it with Jane and they trundled off into the Seven Kings traffic. I headed for a café where I fell into conversation with a group of driving instructors whose pupils were also taking their tests. As a radio blared in the background, apparently playing Bon Jovi on a loop in between news bulletins about the Thatcher leadership challenge, one of the quartet of instructors cheerfully regaled us with a story of how, after a lunchtime drink, and fearing he might be over the limit, he'd tried to outrun the police in his driving school car, with its large sign giving his name and telephone number.

'And do you know what? I was fine,' he said. 'Mind you, they did me for dangerous driving.'

An hour later I emerged to see Morris slumped near the kerb, Jane sitting inside. I tapped on the window. Looking flushed and distracted, she wound it down.

'Well?' I asked.

'I didn't park very near the pavement at the end, so he asked if I wanted him to walk to the kerb,' she said. 'Fortunately he'd told me I'd passed by then. Things are going to change now.'

I leaned into the car and gave her a hug.

'That's true,' I said. 'They're saying on the radio that Mrs Thatcher's resigned.'

Change was in the air. Thatcher was succeeded by the monotone-voiced, monochrome-haired John Major, and I began to wonder about changing Morris, who was looking distinctly tatty. Things came to a head when a front wheel fell off the day after the car had passed its MOT. Morris's front suspension was a 1940s design, with stub axles (the bits that hold the front wheels) attached to the rest of the car by spindles known as 'trunnions', which required regular greasing or they would shear, with calamitous results. I'd failed to grease my trunnions often enough. This sounds like a public school forfeit, and the consequences were certainly painful, although I was lucky to be travelling at walking pace when a trunnion gave up and the car sank on to the tarmac.

I visited a scrapyard, and with my dad helping, made one good piece of front suspension from three dead ones, using two bits of wood and a hammer to straighten the copper washers it contained, then put the car up for sale. It was bought for £100 by a subeditor from New Zealand. She drove Morris from London to Edinburgh, and spent the next year sending us postcards charting their progress, including the time they were hit by a police car, resulting in another insurance payout.

When Morris failed the MOT on fifteen counts and finally ended up in a Scottish scrapyard, his owner (yes, 'his,' there's no way round this) broke the news in a letter posted in a black edged envelope.

'Oh, how sad,' said Jane. As she spoke I noticed that her eyes were glistening slightly.

# Write Off

I became a full-time freelance car writer just as the early 1990s recession hit. Financially the timing sucked and I spent three years barely scraping a living, but I had a feeling that if I didn't make a go of it then as a motoring hack I never would.

I'd got through two non-car jobs. One was news editor on a trade magazine for the meat industry that had a sister title which really was called *The Creative Butcher* (sadly this did not have the strapline 'Incorporating Axe Wielding Maniac Monthly'). The magazine was very old-fashioned, and at the time I lacked the social skills to make a success of the job, so I found a berth as a reporter on a local government magazine, working under a news editor with people skills that were even worse than mine, poor sod. He was small, incredibly neat, and although only 28, sported a pencil moustache that gave him the look of a 1950s Brylcreem model. His speech was slow and precise, but subverted by the occasional malapropism. He lived in Dorking and when the local paper misspelled its name he was outraged.

'We "Dorks" must stick together,' he said, without a trace of humour or irony.

After a year I quit, feeling a bit like a skydiver who wasn't entirely sure if his parachute was working, but had decided to jump anyway.

During this period I got through a series of elderly Mk1 Vauxhall Cavaliers. The Cavalier was basically a German-designed Opel Ascona saloon with a shovel nose. It was conventionally good-looking, well made, very simple and dynamically a big improvement on the wobbly old Marina. Jane called this trio 'Charles the First', 'Charles the Second', and, inevitably, 'Charles the Third'. The first one had been a part exchange sold by a little garage in Wallington. It had been owned and loved by a woman who worked for the Royal School of Needlework.

'It's always been serviced and driven properly,' she said, when I phoned to ask about its provenance.

'I learned to drive lorries in the Army during the War, so I always double-declutch.'

That car was mechanically sweet and had years of life in it, but it was also jinxed. People kept crashing into it. The first accident involved a very old lady in a Talbot Sunbeam, who came over the 'give way' lines of a junction on to the dual carriageway down which we were travelling with my aunt and uncle in the back of the car. We were in the inside lane, and swerved to avoid the trundling Talbot, finally connecting with it in the outside lane.

I watched its driver's wrinkled doll head turn, mouth open, as a small Yorkshire terrier with a bow, little legs cycling, flew from the parcel shelf and vanished into the front footwell as the Cavalier buried its nose into the Talbot's flank, buckling metal and shattering glass. Dog and pensioner were shaken but apparently uninjured; my uncle, who was waiting for heart surgery, did not have a coronary.

Two very young police constables appeared, followed by a deeply tanned middle-aged woman who turned out to be Grandma's daughter.

'You've tried to kill my mother! You were going too fast!' she screeched as the child policemen looked on.

This was too much for my aunt.

'My nephew would never try to kill your mother!' she robustly countered.

As the row raged a small, frail old lady sat unnoticed on a wall, clutching her tiny, shivering dog.

This didn't kill the Cavalier, nor did the teenagers who dropped rocks onto its roof on the M4 motorway. It still worked after a bread van reversed into it when it was parked. I'd been changing a number plate light bulb, so was lightly concussed as the Vauxhall's rump bashed my forehead. This briefly left a 'V-shaped' imprint on it from the raised letters that spelt out 'V-A-U-X-H-A-L-L' across its backside. It was still going after a prison officer bashed into it with his Ford Sierra, but was given the coup de grâce by a builder smashing his Transit van into the boot near Gant's Hill Roundabout.

'I'm always doing that,' he said.

Jane was driving, as I'd put her on my insurance and had taken to lending her the car every other week. I'd arrive at her Ilford bedsit on Friday by Cavalier with flowers and a wine box, then go home on Sunday by train. When I returned the following weekend the wine box tended to be rather emptier than when I'd last seen it.

Jane used the car to drive to the Romford school where she'd started teaching, and when I reclaimed it the following Sunday I'm not sure if the car's departure or mine made her sadder, as its absence meant lumping bags full of marking to work on public transport. This would have been preferable to the whiplash injury she received from the headrest-free Cavalier being rear-ended by the builder.

Charles the Second was mechanically knackered, puffing oil fumes into the cabin as it wheezed along. It made us feel sick, so I sold it to a born-again Christian. He whipped out a small Bible and read a lengthy passage of scripture about sin, then clattered away.

Charles the Third had a bent front wing, and had been

sitting on the roadside near where I lived for months. It looked very clean otherwise, so I stuck a message under a windscreen wiper asking if it was for sale. It had started life as a company car for someone who worked at Vauxhall's HQ in Luton, was sold and then owned by one family. The vendor said she'd visited Bushy Park, forgotten to engage the handbrake and the car had rolled into a fence post. The Cavalier had only covered 70,000 miles, she wanted rid, and yes, would take £150. I wrapped some rope round the bumper, tied the other end of this to a telegraph pole, reversed the car, substantially straightening its buckled front end, then used a G-clamp and two bits of wood to more or less unbend the battered wing. Charles the Third went through the MOT painlessly, proved impregnably reliable and became a long-term companion. It wasn't a Bristol, but it was a good car.

Our relationship was nearly cut short on the junction of the Earls Court and Great West Roads, which I joined with too much vim. The back wheels lost grip, the tail slid pendulously and would not be brought back into line. I watched helplessly as the car slid sideways and some railings whipped past its nose. We didn't hit them, but ended up facing the oncoming traffic. This was a handling quirk of the car, which I subsequently treated with respect.

I was getting better at make do and mend motoring, and had discovered that there was a market for writing about this, first with a banger buyer's guide for *The Big Issue*. This led to one of that magazine's stranger digressions, in the form of a motoring column, which it hoped would attract advertisers. For the first time this gave me access to new press vehicles, and old Cavalier driving would be augmented with shiny, state-of-the-art cars like the Daihatsu Charade, Citroën ZX 1.4 and a diesel Vauxhall Astra. I found it hard to contain my excitement, but the column didn't garner any ads and was duly axed.

However, this provided fresh cuttings and I approached

*The Guardian* with some story ideas. Its motoring editor was a charming man called John Samuel, who was also its skiing correspondent.

'Could you do something about old bangers?' he asked. Thus I got into the national press for the first time and began infrequent but decently paid *Guardian* contributions that did wonders for my profile.

I also started getting regular shifts writing news stories on a weekly business title called *Motor Trader*, owned by the publishers of *Personnel Today*. These began with a week's holiday cover, but since I knew about cars and knew about writing news stories I ended up doing regular freelance shifts, talking to car makers' press officers, including one at Renault called Richard Hammond, whom I liked because he spoke human being rather than corporate bollocks.

The door to the world of motoring writing had seemed nailed shut, and there had been periods when I'd given up on it ever opening, but suddenly I was being drawn into the area of journalism I still desperately wanted to join. I didn't fight it.

One reason for this was that there was more work, people were needed to do it, and the driver of that was Jeremy Clarkson, TV's naughty car-driving Harry Flashman, whose turn on BBC2's *Top Gear* was becoming hugely popular by 1993. I'd hit 30 and found that I could earn quite a decent living writing about cars. A lot of people who don't know Clarkson have expressed opinions about what he's like and what he thinks. Since I don't know him either I have no idea, although I suspect I have a rather more herbivorous view of the world that might meet with his contempt. I also know people like me in part owe their careers to his success.

When *The Daily Telegraph* launched an excellent weekly car supplement edited by a journalist genius called Eric Bailey, it hit exactly the right balance between newspaper and car enthusiast readers. I sent him a list of story ideas.

'Would you write me something about bangers?' said Eric. 'Put in some funny stuff about the old heaps you've driven.'

My story made the supplement's front page and was illustrated by Matt, the paper's brilliant pocket cartoonist. After turning freelance, things had got so bad that at one point that I'd considered giving up writing. To revisit the skydiving analogy, it had felt as if my career was hurtling towards splattered oblivion, and the parachute had opened just in time.

The *Telegraph* supplement chewed words, and I developed a facility for finding angles that would interest people who couldn't give a fig about cars as well as those who liked them. Stories that had rattled around in my head for a decade were suddenly in demand, and I became a regular contributor. Eric finessed my copy and taught me a huge amount without ever making it obvious that he was doing so.

In career terms this was the equivalent of finally losing my virginity, and as the 1990s gathered pace I felt elated and relieved. Curdling frustration became energy and drive. I had a 20-year-old's enthusiasm and a decade's worth of writing experience and ideas – a good combination. The mixed-ability social skills still got in the way sometimes, but not to the same extent, as I'd had a little more practice at being alive.

'I wouldn't mind getting married,' said Jane.

We were in the kitchen of the little terraced cottage she'd bought in rural Essex. She'd wanted to move out of London, and was now teaching in Chelmesford. So I had moved in with her. For a fraction of a second I wondered who she had in mind marriage-wise, then realised that it was me.

We went to visit my mother. It was 1995. The joyously lampoonable John Major was still prime minister, just. Despite an improving economy he seemed hapless, hated by many in his own party for not being Mrs Thatcher, beset by factional misbehaviour on his back benches over Europe and an apparently endless run of Sunday paper-filling sex scandals involving his warring colleagues.

Something called Britpop swam into our consciousness, with artists who seemed as fresh as the 2Tone ska acts had in 1980, channelling, or ripping off The Beatles, The Kinks and in the case of the arch, witty Neil Hannon of the Divine Comedy, Scott Walter. Jane and I wondered if we were too old for pop music, but enjoyed it anyway.

English language-mangling footballer Eric Cantona kicked a fan at Crystal Palace and found himself in court on an assault charge, MG re-emerged with a neat little mid-engined sports car called the MGF. A Korean car maker called Daewoo arrived with a pair of horrid cars based on early 1980s Vauxhall Astras and Cavaliers, but sold and serviced them directly without recourse to conventional car dealers. Many thought this would lead to a car sales revolution, with supermarkets piling in and conventional motor traders going out of business. 'That'll be the Daewoo,' ran as an advertising strapline. Ultimately buying habits didn't change and Daewoo went bust. A case of 'no it won't.'

Meanwhile Vauxhall replaced the Cavalier with the supine Vectra, which Jeremy Clarkson savaged on *Top Gear* for its mediocrity, as the Bonzo Dog Doo-Dah Band's 'I'm Bored' played in the background. This created an enjoyable media frenzy of synthetic and real outrage, and did nothing but good for Clarkson's profile. Lots of people still bought the Vectra, many finding that it was indeed very boring.

As we arrived at my mother's cottage I was no longer a Cavalier driver. Charles the Third had been bought by my friend

David, and I was now piloting a hulking Opel Rekord saloon. This wine red contraption had once been a chauffeur car, had a rusty driver's door, a low mileage and no MOT, so it was cheap. A rust-free door from a breaker's was the same colour and had an electric window, but all the others were hand-wound, so I wired up an extra switch for it on the dashboard and revelled in this luxury feature.

My mother emerged from the undergrowth, tiny and white-haired.

'Oh,' she said. 'It's you.'

We sat in the garden and drank tea from chipped cups. Later we went for a ride in the Opel, my mother sitting in the large front seat, stroking its slightly lurid yellow velour trim.

'Did they use teddy bears for the seat covers?' she asked.

This, on many levels, had been a good day. It wasn't a new dawn, for the next visit might be short and abusive, but my mother had seemed relieved just to have some company, and we saw glimpses of a person I barely knew. Children are by necessity egotists when it comes to their parents, perhaps competing with adult interests, passions and needs that have nothing to do with them. The axis from where I viewed her hadn't really shifted from the nine-year-old who'd been put on the train to Preston when she'd become ill and I had, on some irrational level, resented her absence as if it had been her fault. 'Fault' wasn't an issue. She hadn't chosen to be ill and couldn't control where that illness took her, or the fact that when it asserted itself it became a controlling force that was more important than what she, I, or anyone else thought.

When it was time to leave she said, 'Come back. I'd like that.'

I'd sold the floating shoebox houseboat and was more or less living with Jane. When I was in London I stayed with my dad on his delightfully chaotic houseboat, which, after seventeen years, still wasn't finished.

This ageing little boys' den had the ambience of a floating shed with cooking facilities and a TV. Timber, tools, and half-dismembered bits of electrical equipment were stacked in corners. It smelt of varnish and wood shavings and was something of a bolt-hole from the wider world. The mooring had a small garden which my dad had planted with roses and other hardy plants. You got to the boat from a metal landing stage that had been built by London Weekend Television for a Second World War drama where it had been the centrepiece of a Nazi HQ. It stood over some concrete cladding and next to a willow tree, whose branches brushed against the side of the boat at high tide. This was a beautiful spot, close to Isleworth Ait, an island that was also a nature reserve and bird sanctuary. We'd sit on the deck and watch herons fishing, hear the screech of parakeets during the day and owls hooting at night.

The mooring would have been peaceful but for being directly under the flight path into Heathrow Airport. I've flown over it and been on the ground three minutes later. Still, I'm a boy who likes mechanical things, so I didn't mind the noise.

My dad and I drank too much beer, read, talked, laughed, got on each other's nerves and got to know each other better. This was a small Indian summer of shared company, which we knew would be unhealthy to continue for very long. After all, a wedding was in the offing

We were sitting on the deck on an early spring morning, drinking tea, watching pleasure boats making their way towards Richmond, green water slapping against their hulls. 'I'm getting married,' Dad said.

He'd taken early retirement, was now well into his sixties and had been with the same partner for twenty years. It was a great compliment to him that this was what she wanted. I was delighted for both of them, but also gently gripped by an emotion that I realised was jealousy. I knew this was irrational and unfair. I was an adult and this was the first and only time that feeling had surfaced, which I knew said a great deal about my dad and his partner.

The wedding was a happy, sunny, shared experience. I had to give a speech. People laughed in the right places and it didn't cause offence. Jane and I thought long and hard about a wedding present, eventually settling on that piece of kitchen modernity, a microwave oven. It cost £250.

I'd borrowed a Saab 900 Turbo press car, which was essentially a Vauxhall Cavalier in disguise with rather brutal acceleration and a leather interior. It became the wedding car. As I deposited the happy couple at Heathrow and they headed for a honeymoon in Prague, I realised that my dad had been the first one of us to leave home. Soon it would be my turn.

If this had been a happy journey, the next one I made to my mother was not. Aunt Pat had died and I had to break the news. The Opel's radio/cassette player had packed up and, not wishing to travel in silence, I spent £35 at Halfords on a replacement, fitting it in the car park before carrying on.

As my mother clamped herself to me like a child, bereft beyond words, I felt completely inadequate.

After that the energy seemed to seep out of her, and she became tired and resigned, her spiky, mistrustful anger less apparent than before. I visited during Christmas 1996 with books, a cassette player and a mix of jazz and classical tapes. My mother wanted to know who Tony Blair was.

'I think he's going to be prime minister,' I said.

Despite a persistent cough she seemed in pretty good spirits otherwise, and we listened to Fats Waller, and sat in companionable silence.

Early in the New Year I'd been called up for jury service. As I waited in the court lobby my mobile rang. My mother was dead, and I too slipped into the void that I had been unable to fill for her when I'd come bearing bad news the year before. Life stopped, then began rolling forward again, dragging me along with it, colliding against feelings of loss and guilt. Everything was banal, sluggish and leached of colour. I had no idea when the colour would come back.

# The Italian Job

It's funny the things you remember.

I was halfway up an Italian hillside, on a dirt road made of white dusty soil and fist-sized rocks, sheltered by a scraggy olive tree. Next to me was an elderly Italian man, squinting under a filthy pork pie hat. I could see the folds of his brow glistening with sweat.

It was an early afternoon in May, and hot. Some way below us Siena baked and twinkled under a cloudless sky. We heard a car making its way quickly up the track. It sounded raffish and expensive. Then a Bugatti Type 35, dating from the mid 1920s, burst into view, twitching sideways and scattering stones as its leather-helmeted driver worked a big slim steering wheel. Its light blue open two-seater body, small separate wings and tapering tail had the visual delicacy of a dragonfly, but the Bugatti sounded amazingly modern, more contemporary motorcycle than old car. It was hugely valuable, yet being driven hard as it sped up the hill and out of sight.

Soon it was being followed by a procession of ultra rare period Bentleys, Maseratis and other wheeled exotica, all being piloted with similar verve. As the old man and I watched I realised that he wasn't alone. Strapped into a pushchair and sitting impassively under a floppy summer hat was a toddler. She was presumably a grandchild, whom this elderly car fan had brought along, but all the child had to look at was scrub, because her pushchair had its back to the road.

We were watching the Mille Miglia, an annual road race

made up of the sort of old cars normally seen in museums. Originally run over 1,000 miles from the Italian town of Brescia to Rome and back, the Mille Miglia began in 1927, lasting for another thirty years until a hideous accident killed nine spectators, when Spanish nobleman and playboy Alfonso De Portago's Ferrari 338S ploughed into them on a straight stretch of road. De Portago, who'd ridden horses at Aintree and was a member of the Spanish bobsleigh team at the 1956 Olympics, also died, along with his co-driver Edmund Nelson, and the resultant carnage led to the event's demise.

Twenty years later it re-emerged as a nostalgic road rally for cars built up to 1957. As it's run in Italy, in the summer, the end result is probably now the world's longest street party, involving thousands of people having fun watching an often-priceless old car 'passeggiata' hammering through their towns and villages.

On its seventieth anniversary, *The Daily Telegraph* asked me to follow Roger Saul, founder of the Mulberry leather goods empire, who was taking part in a 1932 Alfa Romeo 8C2300 Spider Corsa. Painted a deep red, its spare, open two-seater body, with swooping separate mud guards and small fin rising from the rear of the coachwork to a pair of spare wheels mounted where the boot would otherwise be, had a visual unity and an unfettered exuberance about it. It was also worth more than my house.

I'd be paired up with a photographer called Mike. Short and stocky, he cheerfully announced that he was 'a control freak.' Saul and his wife Monty had a quietly authoritative charm as they chatted amiably and we made our way across a large rectangular square of white-fronted 1930s buildings in the town of Brescia, where the scrutineers saw the cars before the event started. The mid morning sun was already hot, and the lines of cars shimmered in the dry heat.

'Very Mussolini,' said Roger Saul, looking up at the pompous art deco architecture that surrounded us. Entirely oblivious of their surroundings, a pair of mechanics were ministering to the 8C's elegant engine. When it was new, cars were about progress and modernity rather than anxiety of environmental degradation, and this one's designers had clearly made its engine as a piece of sculpture as well as a thing to power the car. It was a metallic temple to horsepower.

We would be travelling with the two mechanics, one of whom, John, had just turned sixty and was celebrating his birthday looking after the Sauls' 8C. He and his younger colleague Peter seemed to operate in their own universe of in-jokes and technical talk, but both were easy going and friendly. They were driving a boxy Daihatsu 4x4, and I'd be spending a lot of time in the back of it.

Back in England there was about to be a general election. After eighteen years the incumbent Tories appeared fractious, tired and dysfunctional. They were being challenged by the Labour Party, led by a young, slick, permanently smiling politician called Tony Blair, who, untouched by years of being in power, looked like a pretty normal human being.

We'd be on the road for the first time during election night, far away from the febrile atmosphere at home, and Jane promised to keep me posted on developments with phone calls.

The Mille Miglia started on a long tree-lined avenue. Everywhere there were lines of extraordinary cars. Huge Cricklewood Bentleys were nose to tail with 300SL Mercedes, 328 BMWs, 'Birdcage' Maseratis, acres of Bugattis, early Ferraris with open two-seat bodies that from the rear resembled insect thoraxes, and incongruously, a tiny Isetta bubble car.

Soon the chunky Daihatsu was part of a mad caravan of the motoring world's equivalent of the Crown Jewels, The police were clearly enjoying themselves weaving their motorcycles and Fiat Punto patrol cars in and out of processions of cars, steaming up to junctions and crossroads so that the Mille Miglia's contestants were unimpeded. Traffic lights were ignored as the Carabinieri waved competitors thorough.

'They want us to go faster,' said John, as we followed the Sauls' Alfa, bobbing and weaving through the parched countryside. On one ruler-straight road that cut through the middle of a dusty dry valley we shot past a tatty little farmstead. Outside it was a tiny ancient woman swathed in black. She sat, smiled and waved a large grubby handkerchief.

The rest of that day took on the pleasurable hazy blur of dry heat, dust, crowds and flashes of colour as a procession of exotic old cars tore through the Italian countryside, many of their drivers racing in a way that would have got them arrested in Britain, but here was part of the spectacle. Packed in amongst a yowling, roaring hoard we barrelled past a village school and saw small children and their teachers pressed against the school fence, waving flags and cheering.

I've never been very engaged by motorsport. I can appreciate the talent and extraordinary skill that go into it, but as something to watch, gaudily painted cars hurtling round the same racing circuit bends over and over again has never really appealed. The Mille Miglia was different. Many of the cars were works of art, and seeing them out in the open, doing what they were built to do, surrounded by people who loved being part of what was going on, was enormous fun.

We kept going well into the night, by which time Jane was ringing with progress reports about the UK election, where it was clear that the Tories were being annihilated. We were in Verona's main square, passing the Roman amphitheatre that served as the opera house. Outside were props for a production of *Aida*, and a huge wooden sphinx loomed over the cars. My mobile phone glowed and rang. It was Jane.

'Michael Portillo's lost his seat,' she said. 'Now I've seen that I'm going to bed.'

'I'm not getting all the shots I need, so I'm going to hire a car,' said Mike.

Which is how I found myself behind the wheel of a tatty little Opel Corsa with press plates stuck to its sides, being waved through red traffic lights by policemen urging me to keep up with the dusty exotics, as Mike hauled himself out of the passenger window to photograph them.

We converged on Assisi. Its main square was filled with beautiful old cars, whose shapes seemed to compliment the medieval buildings. By now Mike and I had got each other's measure.

'If I piss you off because I am a control freak,' he said, 'tell me.' So I did.

'There! There!' he yelled as we shot past a place he wanted to stop. 'Christ! Stop the bloody car!'

'Control freak!'

It quickly became a running joke to be used when he wasn't barking orders as well as when he was, and the rhythm of a good working relationship quickly established itself. We'd stopped to photograph the cars on a bend in a mountain road which snaked between rocks, scrub, and olive trees when the silence was broken by a distant mechanical howl. Then about a mile away something silver flashed briefly into view before diving behind a clump of trees. It was a mid-1950s Mercedes 300SL, a broad open sports car with fared-in headlamps and a gaping front air intake that resembled the mouth of a surprised sea creature. The car was both brutal and beautiful. The noise it made grew and reverberated until it filled the valley. Finally, less than thirty feet from where we were standing it rushed into the corner, an intense mixture of movement and noise, but its driver, an elderly-looking, tortoise-faced man, seemed utterly calm and was barely working its big cream steering wheel. As the 300SL arrived at the bend's apex and sped away up the writhing, wriggling road, sucking that unearthly screaming noise after it, there was something poised and serene about its progress.

'Did you see who that was?' asked Mike.

'John Surtees?'

Surtees was serial 500cc World Motorcycle Champion between 1956 and 1960, and Formula 1 World Champion in 1964, making him the only man to have taken both two- and four-wheeled titles. Decades later we'd had a brief, private view of his still extraordinary skills. I might not have been a motorsports fan, but I knew that was a privilege.

In Assisi I re-joined the Sauls' service crew. Just outside the city we came across his Alfa moribund by the roadside. A metal stay holding one of the front mudguards to the car had sheared, and finding something that would function as a temporary fix was proving a problem.

'Would this do?' I asked John, proffering my cheap Burton's belt, which much to everyone's amusement made a very effective lash up repair. My belt was still helping to keep the 8C's front wing attached to the rest of the car as Vatican Square passed in a blaze of colour and noise and we began the return leg of the race, heading towards Siena. Just outside it John shouted 'There!' and skidded to a halt.

He ran back to a small road sign standing on a single tubular leg of metal. Hauling it out of the ground he threw it into the back of the car.

'You didn't see that,' he said.

That night he took an angle grinder to the sign, using its remains to fashion something that would hold on to the Alfa's wing rather better than my now blackened and shredded belt. The next day I was back in the hire car with Mike the photographer when we found the Sauls' Alfa, again stopped and silent by the roadside.

'The gear lever's snapped,' said Roger Saul. Most of the long chrome wand was intact, but about three inches of it, including the flying saucer-shaped gear knob, had sheared off, leaving a jagged end that would cut his hand to shreds.

Without quite knowing why I pulled up the hire car's luggage cover, looked at the spare wheel and saw that rather than a spindle with a metal wing nut holding the spare there was a sort of plastic doughnut with a threaded hole in the middle.

It fitted over the remains of the Alfa's damaged gear lever, and lashed in place with acres of gaffer tape kept the car mobile and its driver unlacerated all the way back to Brescia and the finish line, where huge crowds lined the streets and cheered.

As we drank champagne in the red-walled garden of a small hotel, I realised that I had experienced a piece of Italian culture, something that went well beyond a few rich people driving some elderly cars, and that it had been months since I'd felt so engaged or laughed so much. Ten weeks before my mother had died, and I'd been wading through the banal, monumental inertia of grief. I knew that it hadn't finished, and this was necessary and healthy, but spending three days chasing a lot of old cars across Italy had proved that other, less important things in life could be enjoyed without feeling disloyal.

# The Power of Three

I'd wanted to become a motoring journalist and have instead become a journalist who writes about motoring. If anything I'm more interested in what people do with cars, or what human or historical quirks have led to those cars turning out as they have. This is one reason why I've had a slightly weird fascination with Reliant three-wheelers, and why they've kept infiltrated themselves into my life.

After my school-age Reliant Robin hairpin bend terror I'd vowed never to get in one again, but when I was asked to visit and write about the Reliant factory in Tamworth, Staffordshire, I broke that vow with predictably bizarre consequences.

By the mid 1990s the Robin's extreme crudity, wobbly dynamics and steeply declining market meant its makers had gone bust. It wasn't hard to see why. Living standards had risen, and few drivers had need of a car that could be driven on a motorcycle licence. Cars themselves were becoming more technically dense, cleaner, safer and vastly more expensive to design and build. The Scimitar had died, and Reliant's attempt at building a cheap modern sports car, a sort of British Mazda MX-5 precursor, was a good idea but looked like a warthog's foetus.

Yet people were perversely fond of Reliant, and rescue had come in the shape of an ex-Jaguar executive who'd got three-wheeler production going in much reduced circumstances. During the 1970s Reliant's factory buildings had dominated both sides of the A5, a Roman road that runs through Tamworth, with lines of cars parked outside them. Workers had to push half-built three-wheelers across the A5 to the place where they were finished off.

When I arrived just a single, scruffy factory unit was working, staffed by a few grumpy Midlanders.

In the company of Reliant's test driver I was shoehorned into a brand new Robin that had flopped, exhausted, from what passed as an assembly line. Having said that he thought the firm's new boss was 'a nutter', the test driver cranked the little car into life and attempted to engage first gear, which the new stiff gearbox resisted. With a mighty shove and a metallic clang he slammed the car into gear and we lurched into the road. For the first ten minutes that was how every gear was engaged, and I asked if this might, possibly, not be good for the car.

'Nah mate,' said the test driver. 'There's some sharp bits on them cogs. Do that a few times and it knocks 'em off.'

Imagining the newly milled bits of swarf this would create slopping about in the gearbox oil before being mashed into an abrasive paste by the gearbox's internals I noticed that we were picking up speed, as this man mercilessly caned the tight brand new motor.

At 75mph a Reliant Robin screams, vibrates and appears to tug at its single front wheel setting up a side-to-side weaving motion.

'Want a go?' said the test driver as we shuddered to a stop in a lay by. Insinuating myself on to the skinny, headrest-free driver's seat and slamming the car into first with manufacturer-approved brutality we again lurched on to the A5. The Robin felt ancient, with its four-speed transmission, wheelbarrow ride and horrible, nervously twitching steering. It also seemed frighteningly flimsy, more a scourge on wheels than a car. A junction loomed and I put the brakes on, but not a lot happened.

'You've got to press them harder than that,' said the test driver. 'There's no power assistance.'

The Robin was an engineering throwback, still being made in an era of crumple zones, exhaust catalysts, traction control, fuel injection and anti-lock brakes. For the price of a modern supermini you could have a new, near homemade, pre-abused Reliant Robin, without any of these things, or even the same number of gears and wheels. You'd have to be an idiot to want one, and the supply of idiots was drying up.

'What do you think?' asked the test driver.

'Different,' I said, promising myself never to drive one again. What I didn't realise was that my final encounter with a Robin would involve not only driving, but actually owning it.

In France there's a busy industry making tiny low-powered microcars. These are the French equivalent of the Reliant, and can be driven by teenagers and Gallic farming matriarchs without a full car licence. They get in everyone else's way, but at least they have four wheels

I'd sold a story to *Top Gear* magazine about visiting the people who made these weird cars, and the editor, revealing a previously unsuspected sadistic streak, said he wanted me to make the trip in a Reliant Robin.

Reliant was still just about in business, although the ex-Jaguar executive had fled and the latest owners would soon begin to import those French baby cars to Britain. My request to borrow a press Robin was greeted by gales of laughter.

'We don't have any of those,' said the Reliant person, so I bought a second-hand one.

This cost £150 and was being offloaded by a man with a beard. He'd bought it as a cheap way of getting his kids to school, but they'd refused to be seen in it, so when I acquired the car it was being used to store garden rubbish, and was filled with bits of hedge. On the way home I began sneezing and my eyes itched. Hay fever. Driving the bloody thing for 800 miles across France would be a joy.

This Robin was old and tired. A coat hanger kept its farting exhaust from scraping along the tarmac, and for some reason its front wheel was out of alignment and rubbed against the stub axle and steering gear. I took it to Tooting, home of a wonderful organization called Mac Motorcycles, which operated from a cavernous showroom and workshop some way along the high street. It also specialised in Reliants. A man in overalls said my horrid prize wasn't beyond redemption. I booked it in for a few days' time and drove home.

Later, the starter was particularly sluggish. I turned the key again, and instead of a grinding, mechanical churning, there was a soft 'whump' noise, rather like a gas oven igniting. Flames shot out from the engine compartment, licked my trousers and set light to the wiring beneath the dash.

When the fire engine arrived the roof lining was blazing merrily and the windscreen had shattered. Ten minutes later, as we surveyed the sodden, smoldering ruin, the cheerful fireman said dousing self-immolating three-wheelers was still a regular part of his job.

Traffic police are alleged to have called these cars 'plastic pigs,' and with their tiny cramped engine bays they were certainly pigs to maintain. Frequently being the property of broke, ageing and possibly arthritic owners often meant skipped maintenance, so a mixture of arcing from tired sparkplug leads, combined with fuel leaks and a fug of petrol vapour, made external combustion a frequent occurrence, and the cars burnt very well.

'I've seen one of them when all that was left of the body was the gel coat,' said the fireman. 'It was like an eggshell. I touched it and it shattered.'

As the local scrap dealer's lorry arrived and its big mechanical hand grabbed what remained of 'my' Robin and plucked it from the roadside, the fireman smiled broadly as he said.

'And now there's one less.'

# Driving Ambitions

I don't like driving fast or being driven fast. This wasn't what I was expecting when I began writing about cars. It's a case of too much information.

Driving is often a banal process, but it can be elevated with skill and talent. You can see the same thing with elite tennis or football players, who operate on another level of poise and co-ordination.

I've shared press cars with people like racing driver/journalist Mark Hales or Sue Baker, the pre-Clarkson *Top Gear* presenter who wrote for *The Observer* and is still going strong. They can be fast in the right places, and entirely responsible everywhere else, so are neither dangerous nor antisocial. They make a car flow. Every input, from engine speed, gears, clutch, brakes and steering, is smooth and minimal. They don't work hard and the car settles down. The fact that they have seen and anticipated what is going on around it, and are invariably in the right place to get round corners, reduces the huge forces that tug and work at tyres and suspension.

Put me on the same roads and I will be slower, but the car will be working harder. It's a rhythm thing that, mostly, I haven't quite got and is one reason why I was rotten at sport. This doesn't worry me. I'm not a bad driver, I'm an average one with a better-than-average understanding of vehicle dynamics. I know what they are, even if I can't always access them, and know that to try would be dangerous and stupid.

Then there is something my schoolfriend David calls 'the

vanishing point'. I'd helped find him a job as a freelance press car delivery driver. David had been through numerous driving courses, and it amused both of us that he knew more about how cars handled than I did.

'Look up the road as far as you can,' he'd said, as I piloted the ratty MK2 Volkswagen Scirocco coupé that I owned at the time.

'You'll reach a point where your brain freezes the image. As you get closer it will move, so keep looking ahead to where everything appears to stop and then head for it. It'll help your anticipation because you'll see potential hazards sooner, and you'll find that the car is generally in the right place on the road. It's not a failsafe, but it works on corners, unless the corner really tightens up, so you have to be careful.'

I couldn't see this at all, and it took two years and another trip with David before it suddenly clicked.

I'd been asked to write about an old car road rally in Belgium and France for *Classic Cars* magazine and needed an old car. Vauxhall has a fleet of period vehicles, looked after by a charming pair of blokes who'd once worked on the assembly lines that made things like my old Cavaliers.

'We've got a PA Cresta you can borrow,' said the press officer. Dating from the late 1950s, the PA was a scaled-down fake American car with extravagant wrap-around front and rear screens, acres of chrome and fins along its rear wings. Inside was a metal dashboard with chrome switches. The three-speed gearbox employed a clunky steering column change. The lazy, heavy 2.6 litre straight six petrol engine sounded like an elderly British touring coach. The Cresta had two huge squishy bench seats front and rear that were actually very comfortable, vague steering and squishy handling. It wasn't a big fan of corners, preferring to amble along in a straight line, and it was rare, as most of its brethren had been consumed by galloping rust years before. On many levels it was a rotten car, but we loved it.

The rally itself was stuffed with early Triumph TRs, Alfa

Romeos, pre-war Bugattis and a 1930s Talbot with delicate art deco coachwork. Two middle-aged English blokes in a handsome Jaguar XK140 were also competing. One of them seemed to find us hilarious, and when David pointed out that this man was 'trying to take the piss,' I became aware of a constant stream of mildly barbed or derogatory comments about our car, our lack of preparation, my driving. As usual, I hadn't noticed.

'I think that's what's annoying him,' said David.

I discovered that the Vauxhall's sluggish responses matched my own, and for the first time the vanishing point thing swam into focus. We weren't going very fast, because the car wasn't capable of it and anyway, we didn't want to torture the old dear, but we were going pretty quickly for a Vauxhall Cresta. I found the rhythm in driving it that had eluded me in far better, quicker cars, even beating the Jaguar duo on one stage. They weren't laughing after that, and abandoned the rally a day before it ended. David and I crossed the finishing line second to last, delighted with our performance and rather fond of the chrome-grinned, cheerfully vulgar Cresta.

'I won't have a word said against this car,' said David. 'In fact I'd like to take it home.'

I have driven supercars, finding them variously exciting, intimidating and fatuous. The 'rich man's decorative penis sheath on wheels' aesthetic of some, although not all modern Ferraris and Lamborghinis really doesn't do it for me. Whatever their dynamic merits, this attention-seeking excess is a bore. Some supercars are all about the purist engineering. This less-is-more approach influenced the original McLaren F1 road car – once the world's fastest production vehicle. There's nothing bulked up about this car, which does without power steering or power-assisted brakes because it doesn't need them. Nothing is wasted and there is a minimalist purity about it that someone looking at an elegant suspension bridge or even a spider's web might find aesthetically pleasing. The car was the brainchild of an ex-Formula 1 racing car designer, Gordon Murray, whose own transport of choice has been an original rear-engined Fiat 500, and who has spent years trying to get a similarly ascetic city car into production.

Murray also helped with the development of the Honda NS-X from 1989, whose body and suspension bits were made from extruded aluminium, a design first at the time. It was very light, very strong and a piece of industrial art. Some of its complex suspension parts wouldn't look out of place on plinths in an art gallery.

Test drivers included Formula 1 champion Ayrton Senna, and with a mid-mounted 3.0 V6 it was as quick as a Ferrari. I drove one from London to Edinburgh and back to interview the novelist Iain Banks for *Top Gear* magazine. Banks owned a Porsche 911 and wanted the chance to drive a Ferrari, something we arranged as part of the story, borrowing a front-engined 456 GT. Banks' repudiation of cars like this – he ended up driving a Toyota Prius – was still in the future.

The Honda felt infinitely more modern than the Ferrari, which was a younger design. Its driving position was perfect, it was beautifully made and detailed, and it could be driven to the shops or hacked round a racetrack at unfeasible speeds. Its envelope of abilities was enormous, yet there was nothing excessive about the car, and even someone with my blunted responses could sense this. It was great company, whose modern equivalent, I suppose, would be the Audi R8.

I was 34 when I bought a Bristol 401. It was the single most expensive object I've ever owned, an indulgence and a good thing to have got out of my system.

The old car world is like the building trade. There are plenty of chancers and charlatans, but the good people are very good. So before I found my dream car I saw others with paint that appeared to have been applied with a roller, and whose gearboxes sounded like old nuts and bolts being rattled round a biscuit tin. One had a parping exhaust partly held up with an offcut of carpet. The one I eventually bought looked and sounded good but had received a mixed-ability restoration. When I picked it up I was frothing with excitement, but close to tears when it finally arrived home seven hours later on the back of an AA lorry. I'd got the car properly warm, then gently opened it up, at which point it began to overheat. The head gasket had died, which meant an eye-wateringly expensive engine rebuild, where we discovered that the gasket had been fitted upside down, blocking a couple of oil ways and a water channel. Fortunately we'd moved to a Kentish village with a garage in an old forge, run by an ex-Le Mans mechanic, Keith Croucher, who gave me counselling and fixed the car, repeatedly, as things like a driveshaft and the gearbox broke. As I grew poorer and the Bristol got better, Keith and I became friends.

Dating from 1951, the Bristol appeared to have shrunk. My father's 401 had seemed huge; this car did not. By modern standards it had hopeless lights, tiny windscreen wipers that flapped slowly backwards and forwards and brakes that didn't work very well.

And yet the Bristol was a lovely thing to use. Nothing was power assisted, so driving it was an entirely mechanical process, a direct connection between driver and car. The steering in particular had the precision of something that used handcrafted parts. The 2.0 straight six engine, essentially a reconstituted, 1930s-designed BMW unit appropriated in 1945 as war reparations, had its work cut out to power a heavy, sixteen-foot-long car, so the Bristol had to be rowed along by its gear lever, rather like my Citroën Dyane, but it sounded wonderful and possessed a free-revving lightness that belied its years.

In part I'd bought the Bristol to rewind life to a place that no longer existed, and while it re-awakened pleasant nostalgia, I began to appreciate it for what it actually was rather than what I'd imagined it to be. It was the product of human creativity, a piece of uncompromised design that had a slightly caddish elegance because its rounded coachwork had been designed to cleave the air efficiently. The Bristol was probably one of the best cars of its era, but it was also a labour of love.

Driving it has the quality of flying an old piston-engined aircraft along the ground. You are serenaded by its engine's thoroughbred dog growl, air buffeting through the open driver's door window, as you look down the long tapering bonnet at the outside world and constantly finesse and adjust its controls. Modern cars are often passive, but not the Bristol. It demands complete engagement to get the best from it, and you share the experience with it. I suspect steam engine drivers will know the feeling too.

'You smell of Bristol,' said Jane after a summer drive that had lightly perfumed my clothes and hair with the scent of wood, leather and hot oil. 'I quite like it,' she added.

As a child I used to think that my dad's Bristol was alive. I don't see mine in the same way; not quite, but it is one of the most animate inanimate objects I have ever encountered.

The Bristol arrived at about the time that I'd begun freelancing as commissioning editor for a weekly motoring supplement launched by the *London Evening Standard*. This meant returning to a Fleet Street editorial office for the first time since my messenger boy days – although to be pedantic the paper had by then decamped to Kensington. Gone were the noise of manual typewriters and the swirl of fag smoke. There were more women and not all the faces I saw were white. My boss, motoring editor David Williams, was also chained to the news desk, working to deadlines that made me sweat just thinking about them, so I had to run more of the supplement then either of us had imagined. This was a mixed blessing for David, but fantastic for me. He was operating on a different level from anything I'd experienced, and to survive in his company I had to improve fast. It was just what I needed.

The *Standard* was edited by Max Hastings at the time, and news seemed to be his particular passion, so it was fascinating watching him at work. The car supplement, *ESWheels*, was hardly a priority to Hastings, but it was a new launch and an exciting thing to be involved with. I developed a features list from scratch, commissioned people I'd admired for years, and others I came to admire even it if wasn't always for their writing. Seeing some of their words in a raw state was instructive, and made me feel better about my earlier excesses. Editing their work taught me a lot too.

I found a way to spike a story about teenagers getting motorcycle training that was actually an attack on the parenting style of the author's ex-husband and his purchase of a motorcycle for their son. The piece praising an economy device written by an ex-Fleet Street old hand who'd failed to mention that he was also acting as the firm's PR consultant got the bullet too. I said no to offers of car poetry, and when an alleged scooter journalist phoned and told me firmly that I should give him a job because he'd read our coverage of the subject and had thought 'did they pay for that?' I managed not to tell him to fuck his crash hat.

We used people who couldn't write but knew stuff, and journalistic pros who knew how to find out things, and some who had both skills. Mike Smith, the DJ, was a contributor and so, rather bizarrely, was LBC Radio's Nick Ferrari. Brian Sewell, a lovely man whose complete lack of arrogance when dealing with the paper's production staff came as a revelation, was supposed to write a feature on ugly cars, but never quite got round to it.

I could have been kinder to one or two prima donnas, perhaps because their insecurities weren't entirely unfamiliar, but I knew just how gut-churning it could be for a work-from-home journalist to ring up a commissioning editor and try selling a story. I hope nobody felt furious or three inches tall after their encounters with me.

There were TV screens on the news floor, and I came back from lunch to see people gathered round them looking at a tower block with a gaping hole in its side.

'It's the World Trade Center,' said Mike Stone, the subeditor who looked after our supplement. He'd edited John Diamond's and James Cameron's copy, but knew more about cars that I did and liked our little supplement. We looked at the wounded skyscraper.

'A plane's flown into it,' said Mike.

I assumed this was a light aircraft. Of course it wasn't. This was 11 September 2001.

We watched the replay of a jet slamming into one of the towers. Only it wasn't a replay. This was a live feed and we'd seen the second aircraft as it struck the other tower. When I realised this it felt as if iced water was cascading down the inside of my ribcage.

'Is this the biggest news story ever?' said Mike.

Within half an hour Hastings and his colleagues had calmly pulled the paper to pieces and filled it with the biggest news story ever. This was journalism at its absolute best.

There were rumours of jets heading for London and other

capital cities, and an atmosphere of awed panic as the afternoon wore on. When one of the towers collapsed I turned away from the screen. Knowing then that what I was seeing was happening at that moment I thought of the people trapped inside it.

I spent two years at the *Standard*, working with everyone from the absurd to the absurdly talented (or both), and enjoyed it enormously. In fact I loved it, and only wish I'd enjoyed it more, because it couldn't last. The internet was about to chew into the print media, and when Max Hastings left, his replacement looked at our supplement's bottom line, found it wanting, and pulled the plug.

I returned to life as a journalist who sells stories rather than commissions them, finding the process as nerve-racking as ever, but knew professionally I'd had the ride of my life, and that I'd come a long way.

It seemed that at last I was ready, and had learned.

# The Knowledge

When I was thirteen I wanted to be a freelance motoring journalist who drove cars for a living and authored a column where I could write what I liked about them.

Despite some often self-inflicted obstacles and diversions, that is, more or less, where I have ended up, and I'm very grateful. I've been helped and shown enormous kindness and forbearance by family, friends and colleagues and learned a huge amount from them. I've been given wonderful assignments, met some fascinating people and gone to some extraordinary places through my job. I've driven cars that have been exotic, interesting, occasionally dire and often deeply boring. And I have been paid to do all this.

But I am no longer thirteen and I do not see the world in the same way. I believed that there was human creativity in cars that were often very ordinary, and can still contemplate this without embarrassment now. It was there if you looked hard enough for it. Perhaps I was looking for humanity in the character of these things because I was less sure-footed when it came to dealing with people themselves. On a bad day that's still true, but now that I'm officially middle-aged I can contemplate it without embarrassment too. I still have a lot to learn about people, which is actually a gift, just as I know that as a writer, there is still room for improvement. It's a real joy to be well into a career knowing that you are still learning and developing.

Cars may be the things I mostly write about, but they are not why I write. The writing itself has become more important and cars have become an adjunct to it, and an adjunct to life rather than its purpose.

Which is why when Jane and I were married and we were driven away from the church in the Bristol, its character was part of what made the day special; its presence was important but entirely ephemeral.

I was once asked in a radio debate about the evils or otherwise of motoring, whether I loved my car.

Resisting the temptation to ask 'In what way?' I said, 'No. I *like* my car, but I love my wife.'